AMERICA'S ARCHITECTURAL

ROOTS

AMERICA'S ARCHITECTURAL ROOTS

ETHNIC GROUPS THAT BUILT AMERICA

Building Watchers Series

EDITED BY DELL UPTON
NATIONAL TRUST FOR HISTORIC PRESERVATION

THE PRESERVATION PRESS

The Preservation Press
National Trust for Historic Preservation
1785 Massachusetts Avenue, N.W.
Washington, D.C. 20036

Printed in the United States of America
90 89 88 87 86 5 4 3 2 1

Library of Congress Cataloging in Publication Data

America's architectural roots.
    (Building watchers series)
    "National Trust for Historic Preservation."
    Bibliography: p.
    Includes index.
    1. Ethnic architecture — United States.
2. Vernacular architecture — United States.
I. Upton, Dell. II. National Trust for Historic
Preservation in the United States. III. Series.
NA705.A485 1986 720'.973 86-25165
ISBN 0-89133-123-9

Dell Upton wishes to thank the following persons for their assistance with this book: Simon J. Bronner, Jean-Claude Dupont, George Ellis, Gene Itogawa, Karen Kevorkian, Carol Krinsky, Bonnie Loyd, Howard Wight Marshall, Willard B. Moore, David Murphy, Allen G. Noble, Jerry Pocius, Orlando Ridout V, David Sokol, William H. Tishler, Rudolph J. Vecoli, Richard Vidutis, John Michael Vlach and Lauren Weingarden.

Edited by Diane Maddex, editor, and Gretchen Smith, associate editor, The Preservation Press

Designed by Anne Masters, Washington, D.C.

Composed in Trump Mediaeval by General Typographers, Inc., Washington, D.C.

Printed on 70-pound Frostbrite by the John D. Lucas Printing Company, Baltimore, Md.

Contents

Introduction

The diversity of North America's landscape has fascinated travelers since the 17th century. Even today the veneer of commerce cannot conceal the variety of houses, farms, villages and even cities that distinguish New England from the West, Iowa from Nebraska, northern California from southern California. Differences in climate, topography and resources account for some of this regionalism, but much that enriches the American scene reflects the ethnic identity of its builders.

Ethnicity permeates American political, social and economic life. Although it has been closely studied since the 19th century, its precise nature and meaning remain controversial. The word *ethnic* is derived from a Greek term that means people in general but that also implies outsider. It was coined by scholars at a time when many Americans believed that there was a common or standard American culture. This they equated with Anglo-American tradition. People who departed from the standard culture — especially members of national groups who had immigrated since the Civil War — were ethnics. *Ethnic* still suggests otherness, even though Americans now realize that their culture is and ought to be much less homogeneous than the old interpretation suggested. To the extent that they do have a common national culture, it is the international popular culture developed throughout the Western world in recent centuries, rather than an outgrowth of a single nation's traditions.

For this book *ethnicity* can be defined simply as the shared cultural patterns that unite one group and distinguish it from others in the larger society. It is an expression of common experience based on race, nation, language or religion, or more often some combination of these. It is typically an accident of birth, although some people argue that it can be adopted voluntarily as well. As an example they point to the Mormons, people of many national backgrounds who voluntarily adopted a new religious doctrine and based a distinctive way of life on it in their Great Basin homeland.

How is ethnicity expressed in architecture? The answers given depend on one's assumptions. If ethnicity is the expression of common experience, then blacks, Asians, Native Americans and Anglo-Americans belong in *America's Architectural Roots* because by our definition they are no less ethnics than the Czechs, Hispanics, Ukrainians and other groups whom we might expect to find in a book about ethnicity.

A second assumption relates to the vantage point from which one views ethnic architecture. From outside the United States the American setting seems undifferentiated and unimportant compared with the foreign heritage. Looking in we would ask what we could find here that looks like Denmark or Germany or Japan. This approach presumes that ethnic cultures stopped developing when people arrived at Ellis Island or Angel Island. Anything that happened subsequently was uninteresting. Historically, the exterior stance has defined native peoples as the Indians — a group that existed only collectively, as the opponents of European cultures. In these essays our point of view is different. This is a book about buildings that were constructed in America, and not in Denmark, Germany or Japan. There are several important reasons for looking beyond simple survivals of foreign cultures to understand American ethnic architecture.

Immigrants' motives varied. Some left their homes because they could no longer make a living, others because they were enticed by opportunities. Some found the political or religious atmosphere in the home country oppressive; others found it attractive in their new homes. Whatever their personal motives, they were also part of a larger phenomenon. Their dislocation was the product of a vast economic and social transformation of the Western world that began in the 16th century and quickly drew in Asia and Africa. The Spanish conquerors, the Pilgrims and Puritans and later the Germans, Irish, Italians and Chinese were part of it; these great migrations have yet to end. Although the names for their troubles varied, all emigrants found themselves pushed out of their traditional places and seeking new ones in other locales. Many made modest changes, moving from the countryside to the city, or from one country to an adjacent one, before deciding on a more drastic relocation. Even then the United States was not the only choice. Asians moved to Africa and elsewhere in Asia; Europeans chose Africa, Asia, South America or Australia as well as North America. For most emigrants, environment was more important than government. Thus, we ignore national borders when considering the Ukrainians and German-Russians who chose the Great Plains of the United States and Canada and the Spanish and Mexicans of northern Mexico and the southern United States.

We must emphasize the American setting for another, even more important reason. The experience of foreign-born Americans included their lives in America as well as in the homeland. In their first years here, many immigrant ethnic groups did reproduce some of what they had known at home, because that was all they knew. But as they grew familiar with the new environment, society and economy, they adjusted to their setting. This does not mean that they necessarily abandoned what they had known before, although that was possible. Many chose to see the new through old eyes, developing a landscape that combined both in distinctive ways. They built differently from other Americans but also diverged noticeably from what they had known at home. However, other American ethnic traditions had no recognizable foreign antecedents. This is obviously true of Native American architecture. It may be true as well of the brick-veneered log houses that Charles Calkins and William Laatsch describe. They are unknown in Belgium, but we call them Belgian because they were built almost exclusively by Belgian immigrants in Wisconsin.

It is clear that we can expect American ethnic building traditions to blend memory and experience in varying proportions. So far most scholarly attention has been given to the domestic and rural traditions where memory has dominated. Family structures tend to change slowly and to be tied to particular patterns of domestic spaces as well. For this reason, dwellings built by ethnic families are distinctive and relatively easy to identify. Changes in them are definite, if not always easily interpreted, signs of transformation in an ethnic group's most private life. Consequently, all the essayists in *America's Architectural Roots* discuss living spaces.

Agricultural systems are nearly as distinctive. Farming is by nature intensely localized. The crops grown depend on variations in soil and climate. Farmers develop farm buildings and farmstead plans to accommodate their particular customs. Traditional farmers who emigrated to America typically sought soils and climates similar to those with which they were familiar, built traditional agricultural structures and attempted to farm as they did at home. But the environmental sensitivity of agriculture worked against them. Some farmers simply shifted to the locally dominant agriculture and its architectural envelope. They demolished their traditional farm buildings or adapted them to the new farming. Where ethnic farmers were among the first settlers in their area, as the Germans were in Pennsylvania and Wisconsin, their native practices contributed to the shaping of a new local agriculture. In the process they frequently combined old architectural concepts with others developed or borrowed in the new land and along the way created innovative American ethnic buildings. An example is the Pennsylvania forebay or bank barn, a hybrid of traditional German mixed-use, bank-sited barns and English ideas about barn planning and use. It was an American type that for a century and a half served farmers of all ethnic backgrounds in Pennsylvania and its cultural provinces.

Landscapes of experience are more numerous and more important than the architecture of memory. Not only did the American environment contribute to the new mixtures that gave each region its distinctive flavor, but different resources for building were equally critical. The abundance of wood in the eastern forests allowed 17th-century English settlers to rejuvenate a frame-construction tradition that was dying for lack of trees in Britain. On the other hand, knowledge of wooden building was of little use to 19th-century people who settled on prairies with few trees.

Although exploration of the landscape of experience has lagged, we can identify examples where experience dominates and even eradicates memory among the groups included in *America's Architectural Roots.* Africans came from a variety of locales and cultures, but in America they were treated as a single, separate group and developed common responses to widely shared living conditions. Slaves in Chesapeake quarters held distinctively Afro-American attitudes toward personal territory and patterns of spatial use that spoke less of Africa than of surviving in America. Similarly, Chinese on the West Coast created urban patterns that grew out of restrictions on immigration, the importation of families, ownership of property and residence. As Christopher Yip shows, by the early 20th century most Chinese were confined to urban ghettos where they lived in buildings constructed and owned by non-Chinese. Yet, we can identify patterns of residence and spatial use that emanated from this all-male, transient society. Furthermore, the companies, or ethnic associations, that bound immigrants to kin and obligations at home were novel institutions that grew out of the overseas Chinese experience.

Experience permits choice. Ethnicity is cultural, not genetic. It consists of ideas that people learn from one another, and these ideas can be expressed or not according to individual choice. Some people prefer to ignore their ethnic ties, while others' experience creates a desire for self-assertion and the strengthening of bonds. They protect cherished traditions in the face of change. Other ethnic expressions are brand new — invented traditions, as historian Eric Hobsbawm calls them. Invented traditions are customs made up out of whole cloth or created by transforming marginal or half-forgotten traditions into something flamboyant and conspicuous. For example, many of the lively costumes worn by European ethnics on festive occasions were invented in the 19th century by people who regretted the passing of peasant life.

Architecturally, invented traditions are often evident in religious buildings. Religious institutions are favorite settings for maintaining ethnic bonds, and ethnic groups frequently build places of worship that are architecturally reminiscent of their homelands. But it is noteworthy that these buildings tend to distill native architectural features into an idealized representation of the old country. Not all invented architectures are religious. The colorful architecture of America's Chinatowns and Japantowns and the lodges and assembly halls built by European ethnics represent the voluntary transformation of traditional forms into something different from historical examples. They may not have the sanction of history behind them, but they are useful to their builders as valued expressions of personal bonds.

The Spanish colonial revival buildings discussed by Kathleen Deagan and Joe Graham take experience another step beyond memory. In Spanish colonial buildings, idealized and abstracted architectural forms of one ethnic group were appropriated by another for entirely modern reasons. Similarly, the amalgamation of Japanese and native Hawaiian forms in Hawaii represents a conscious attempt by architects to create a Hawaiian architecture that would symbolize the cultural synthesis that has taken place in the islands. In both instances the builders sought to create artificially the kind of regionalism they recognized in those less calculated ethnic landscapes.

America's Architectural Roots draws together essays on 22 ethnic architectural traditions, written by leading authorities on each. It should be clear by now that ethnic experience, and the resulting ethnic architecture, is as varied as the groups themselves; thus, no single theoretical approach has been followed by all the authors. Rather, each discusses the issues that seem most pressing and the architectural and landscape forms that seem most important according to the results of his or her own research.

This approach extends to the definitions of ethnic groups, which have also varied on a case-by-case basis. For example, African and Native American builders both came from varied tribal and cultural backgrounds. It is occasionally possible to attribute an isolated architectural survival to a specific African background, and John Vlach has shown that the core of the shotgun house is probably Yoruban. However, Afro-American experience created an Afro-American architecture that is nationally uniform and is most fruitfully treated as a single entity. On the other hand, the architecture of the 300 Native American tribal groups mentioned by Peter Nabokov and Bob Easton has been grouped geographically and culturally. *Pueblos, tipis,* longhouses and other regionally distinctive Native American architectures are the product of environment, religion and intergroup contact much as immigrant ethnic architecture was.

European ethnic architecture might be classified by regional cultures as well. Readers will notice that the name for the main room of German, Norwegian and Swedish houses — the *Stube, stue* and *stuga,* respectively — is the same, which is a clue that northern European architectural traditions transcended national and linguistic boundaries. Several authors claim that their own groups were instrumental in introducing log building to North America. These attributions are not evidence of competition among writers but reflect the remnants of a common peasant culture shared by many Europeans as late as the early 20th century. House types, farm buildings and farmstead plans followed large patterns that could be traced from England to eastern Europe. Log building originated in south-central Europe several thousand years ago. It spread northeast as far as present-day Finland and Russia. Many immigrants to North America knew some version of it. While there were regional variations in log building in Europe, the traditions were similar enough that they could easily be combined here. As a result, American log building is an ethnic hybrid that has been nearly impossible to sort out.

Nevertheless, it has seemed more reasonable to divide European groups nationally rather than by cultural categories. Most immigrants since the Revolution have been motivated by nationalistic as well as cultural impulses; political jurisdictions are an important part of their self-definition.

Our American viewpoint led us to organize *America's Architectural Roots* into three sections, based on periods of immigration; within these periods, groups are arranged alphabetically. The first section includes the Native Americans and Native Hawaiians, whose settlement preceded Afro-European colonization by intervals ranging from several centuries to thousands of years and whose architecture can therefore be considered indigenous.

The second section includes groups whose most significant immigration preceded the American Revolution. Most were western Europeans or Africans, and most were the first colonists in their localities. Many settled in remote areas and typically preserved their ethnic architectural traditions longer than post-Revolution immigrants. Their numbers were small when compared with 19th-century immigrants, but their role in shaping subsequent American landscapes was often disproportionate to their population.

The final, post-Revolution, section is dominated by the great wave of immigrants who arrived in the United States between the mid-19th century and World War I. Their origins were worldwide. They were as likely to move to the cities as to the countryside, to use standard American buildings as to construct traditional ones from their homelands. Most were surrounded by people of other origins. Lacking geographic insulation, they expressed their ethnicity in a more selective and more conscious way.

Of course, these divisions are crude ones. The Irish, for example, were equally significant, for different reasons, in the colonial and national periods, and most groups could identify at least a few members who immigrated at every period of American history. Two of the European groups demanded subdivision. The histories of the Spanish Caribbean and Mexico were very different, and their American architecture shows this. Similarly, the Germans who came to the Midwest and Texas in the 19th century were set apart from their 18th-century Rhenish predecessors on the East Coast by European regional origins, American settlement environments, religion and post-Renaissance popular architectural ideas.

America's Architectural Roots is the largest compilation to date of the architecture of ethnic America. Yet, it treats only 22 traditions, while the monumental *Harvard Encyclopedia of American Ethnic Groups* includes discussions of 113 foreign groups, plus Hawaiians, Native Americans and several other ethnicities indigenous to the United States. Moreover, in this book some well-known and conspicuous ethnic groups, such as the Italians, the Greeks, the Poles and the Jews are absent. Why is that? There are several reasons, some having to do with ethnic traditions themselves and more with the state of scholarship. Architecture and landscapes have not always seemed the most appropriate or desirable expressions of ethnicity. Large urban ethnic groups evidently built little that was distinctive but instead expressed their ethnicity through language, food customs, religion and social organizations.

We cannot be too confident in making such assertions, however. The absence of urban ethnic architectures may be more apparent than real. The study of ethnic building traditions is relatively new, and many groups simply have not been investigated. We know, for example, that Estonians, Latvians and Lithuanians built farms that still stand in the Midwest, but no one has examined them. The work that has been done has concentrated on rural groups that settled in close proximity to one another and that constructed easily identifiable folk buildings, creating what Allen Noble has called *ethnic islands*. Yet, we have seen that ethnic expression may be more subtle and more diffuse, and we are only learning to ask about these less conspicuous traditions. The example of the Chinese suggests that urban ethnic landscapes are foremost among these. Some work has been done. Margaret Byington's 1910 study of Homestead, Pa., and more recently Lizabeth Cohen's article on the decoration of early 20th-century urban immigrants' houses, Robert Teske's essay on Greek-Philadelphia home furnishings and Shalom Staub's study of Middle Eastern restaurants come to mind. For the most part, however, urban ethnic landscapes await attention.

In two senses, then, *America's Architectural Roots* is an introduction to the ethnic landscape of America. It will introduce readers to the buildings of a wide variety of groups, from Afro-Americans to Ukrainians. At the same time we hope that it will provoke readers to study the architecture of people who are not included. If the second edition of this book is twice as long, the effort will have been worthwhile.

Dell Upton

NATIVE AMERICANS
Peter Nabokov and Bob Easton

Native American architecture is often reduced to three
stereotypes: the arctic *igloo,* the woodlands *wigwam* and
the plains *tipi.* In reality, the approximately 300 native
groups in North America created a rich variety of
structures. Following designs and construction customs
handed down for centuries, their various structures —
dwellings for different seasons, religious and council
chambers, storage and work enclosures — were arranged in
a wide range of settlement patterns that proved remarkably
consistent over time. In Native American enclaves across
the United States many of these building traditions, often
in altered form, remain alive today.

The outward appearance of Native American dwellings
and settlements resulted from an interplay of forces:
available construction materials, climatic conditions,
technological inclinations, social and political
organization, subsistence strategies, cross-cultural
experiences, religious beliefs and world views. No single
factor dominated everywhere. Yet, careful study of the
ecological settings, mythological prototypes, construction
methods, use patterns and encoded symbolism for a given
building can reveal which influence predominated in each
case.

Social customs, for example, clearly shaped the most
striking characteristic of Iroquois buildings — their extreme
length — while the varied food-gathering habits of the
Great Lakes people were perhaps the predominant reason
for the notable quantity of structures in their architectural
inventory. Conflict with the Spanish caused many Pueblos
to seek defensible town sites on inaccessible mesa tops, in
defiance of their practical need for available drinking water
and firewood. The uniformly widespread design of the
arctic winter house, whether made of snow blocks or whale
bones and sod, was dictated by the harshest habitat on the
globe.

Each tribe put its stamp on its house culture, but it is
sometimes convenient to categorize Native American
architecture by the anthropological concept of culture
areas. Within the United States six broad regions with
distinctive architectural traditions can be identified: (1)
Eastern Woodlands–Great Lakes, (2) Southeast, (3) Great
Plains–Plateau, (4) Southwest, (5) California and (6) Arctic–
Northwest Coast.

Eastern Woodlands–Great Lakes

One basic construction system served the forested and
riverine world from the Atlantic Ocean to the Great Lakes,
from the Canadian border to the Tidewater region and the
Cumberland River: Frames of saplings lashed together with
fiber cords were covered with bark flats or sewn-reed mats
or both. The appearance, size, permanence, use patterns
and meanings of buildings based on this system varied
considerably, however.

Central Atlantic Algonkian-speaking coastal tribes lived
in the summer in farming villages situated along streams.
During the spring and fall they regularly forayed into the
deeper woods on hunting trips and along the coast for clams
and fish. At the more permanent locations they occupied

Algonkian village of Secota, N.C., drawn by John White in 1585. The dwellings have vertical walls and barrel roofs, with front mats removed for ventilation. (Smithsonian Institution)

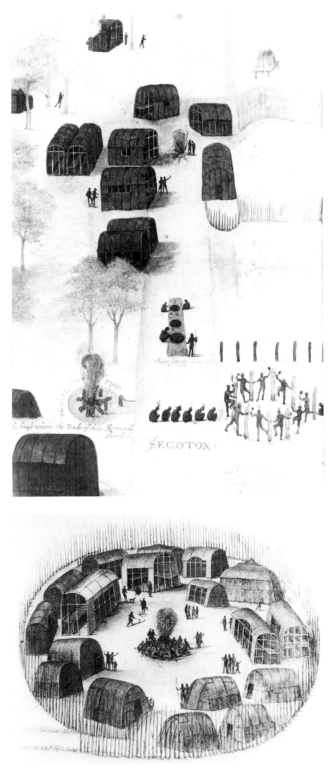

Pomeioc, N.C., another Algonkian village pictured by John White in 1585. Eighteen mat-roofed structures were grouped around a central plaza, all encircled by a pointed stockade. (Smithsonian Institution)

Santee Dacotah village, Great Lakes region, drawn by Seth Eastman about 1850. Summer houses were gable roofed and bark covered.

Quapaw summer lodge, recorded by Robert O. Sweeney in 1860. These large, gabled structures could hold 200 persons. (Minnesota Historical Art Collection)

multifamily structures with barrel roofs, but for shorter trips they transported rolled-up reed roofing mats for use on simple bent-wood frames, which might be left standing for future use. These domical single- or two-family smaller structures are true *wigwams*, a term derived from an Algonkian word for "dwelling."

Settlement patterns might vary within a small area. In North Carolina, for instance, one 1585 village recorded by watercolorist John White was surrounded by a circular stockade, its straight-walled, barrel-roofed multifamily longhouses clustered around a central plaza. Then White drew another community located only a three days' walk away but which had sizable barrel-roofed buildings lining a main thoroughfare that branched into special ritual arenas and lacked a protective palisade.

North of the corn-growing belt, from Maine into Canada's maritime provinces, Algonkian hunters set up conical frames of fir poles rigidified with hoops of short sticks. For covering, birch-bark flats sewn together with spruce root into lengthy scrolls and stiffened at the ends with cedar battens were draped shawl-like around the pointed frame. Interwoven sweet-smelling spruce boughs made a springlike flooring.

Another Algonkian woodlands tradition was found in the Great Lakes region, whose tribes — including some Siouan-speakers as well — perpetuated their house forms long after their East Coast linguistic cousins had been wiped out, removed or acculturated. Their diversified food supply and seminomadic life called for a spectrum of structures. In winter they had the choice of both single and extended domical *wigwams*, plus single and extended conical *wigwams*, to suit the ever-changing needs of

Example of a Chippewa house, a wigwam frame covered with birch-bark mats sewn with spruce root. (Field Museum)

Iroquois longhouse. (Bob Easton)

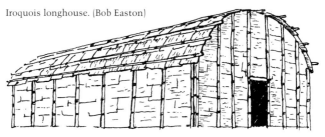

fluctuating population, diverse raw foods to process and mobility. All were sheathed in assorted barks — birch, elm or chestnut —or cattail mats or had reed-mat side walls with birch bark on top for optimal heat containment. These coverings were lashed to the interior frame and then further secured with leaning poles or an exoskeleton of bent saplings to clamp in the mats.

Sweltering summers saw extensive use of cooking and sleeping arbors but also of spacious, gabled-roof buildings that allowed cooling shade and ventilation. Lighter pole constructions sheltered such activities as hide tanning and maple sugaring. Great Lakes religious festivals called for additional special structures and spaces. The largest was the medicine lodge, whose wickerwork extended *wigwam* enclosure, over 100 feet long, was said to symbolize Lake Superior; inside, celebrants enacted migration legends. The smallest was the booth-sized "shaking tent" used for shamanic divination.

Between eastern and western Algonkian worlds lay the domain of the five federated Iroquois tribes in upper New York State. Their year-round longhouse figured prominently in both their mythology and their social organization. The tradition of a husband moving into his wife's home might necessitate gradual extensions of a clan's dwellings until these elm bark–covered structures reached 400 feet in length. These buildings would be regularly aligned in towns protected by elaborate long palisades and ramparts. Today, Iroquois grange-style meeting halls that function as part temple, part forum for religious and social gatherings are proudly referred to as longhouses.

Southeast

Earthworks were the earliest architectural characteristic of the damp woodlands extending south of the Appalachians from the Atlantic Ocean to the Mississippi River and including the subtropical Gulf Coast and the Florida peninsula. Prehistoric societies that matured in the Ohio and Mississippi valleys worshiped and conducted public affairs in spaces marked by four types of earthworks: ridge embankments, burial mounds, effigy mounds and platform mounds.

The Poverty Point site in the southern Mississippi Valley features the first three. Construction here began around 1400 B.C. and at its peak featured six concentric embankments shaped from tons of earth transported in basketfuls to the site. Conceivably the banks held modest, thatched dwellings. Also associated with Poverty Point's elaborate arena were bird-shaped mounds and earthworks enclosing the cremated remains of dignitaries.

The later Adena and Hopewell prehistoric cultures of the Ohio and Illinois valleys elaborated on this architectural base. Around 1000 B.C. the Adena peoples began using log crematoriums that, once burned, were buried beneath conically shaped mounds. Adena domestic architecture was a simpler affair, with wattle-and-daub walls and interior support posts for their thatched roofs. From A.D. 300 to 600 the Hopewell tradition refined its geometrically precise ridge mounds to enclose presumed ritual open-air arenas, represented most elegantly at such sites as Marietta, Newark and High Bank, Ohio. The ongoing effigy mound tradition depicted bears, panthers and reptiles —possibly totemic insignia for social groups.

Thriving between A.D. 750 and 1450, Mississippian culture represented the summation of mound-builder civilization. Continuous Mexican influence evident ever since Poverty Point times now combined with indigenous traditions to produce immense platform mounds, truncated for supporting royal residences or temples that safeguarded sacred fires tended by a priestly class. Cahokia, located outside present-day St. Louis, was the Mississippian metropolis, while its vassal villages extended to the Aztlan site in Wisconsin and Spiro Mounds in Oklahoma. A city of some 50,000 citizens, Cahokia's centerpiece was Monk's Mound, which stood 100 feet high with a 1,037-foot base and loomed over hundreds of lesser mounds.

When De Soto traversed the Southeast from 1539 to 1542, Native Americans were still using sun temples, public plazas, ballgame courts and burial mounds, but the grander cities had almost disappeared. Thereafter, only the Natchez nation, near the mouth of the Mississippi, perpetuated pure Mississippian culture; it was destroyed by the French in the early 1700s. Yet, descendants of this architectural heritage — the historic Creek, Cherokee and Choctaw peoples — continued to perpetuate their ancestral symbols and building forms. They created miniature mounds and every summer held sacred fire rituals in open-air ceremonial "square grounds," which were surrounded by shed-roofed, wattle-and-daub walled arbors. Although their dwellings were simple thatched rectangular buildings, each of their established towns featured a central rotunda

Cherokee village of Takoua in 1797, as seen by a French traveler touring the Tennessee and Kentucky areas. The log houses were built with small logs and chinked with earth and sand. (Smithsonian Institution)

Aerial drawing of a serpent mound
(800 B.C.–A.D. 400), near Peebles,
Ohio, built by the Adena people.
The 600-foot-long mound portrays
a snake figure swallowing a turtle.
(Smithsonian Institution)

Temple and cabin, Acolapossa
village, north of New Orleans,
drawn by a French engineer in
1732. The temple was framed in
poles and roofed with cane mats;
the cabin had wattle-and-daub
walls with a mat roof. (Smithsonian Institution)

John Jumper's Seminole camp,
Cow Creek, Fla., in 1908. A typical
chickee camp such as this is made
of pole and thatched shelters
arranged by single or extended
families. (M. R. Harrington,
Museum of the American Indian,
Heye Foundation)

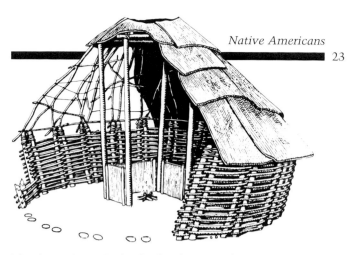

Adena house, Cowan Creek, Ohio, based on postmold excavations. The structures averaged 30 feet in diameter with outward-leaning posts paired to hold horizontal laths. The roof shown is speculative.

or "hot house" for holding winter rituals and councils and housing the elderly and indigent. In the rotunda — as with the square grounds, its summer counterpart — men were assigned seats according to tribal status and rank.

The territory in eastern Oklahoma where these southeastern tribes were relocated in the 1830s today features secluded square grounds where ancient rituals are still performed by some of these same tribes, but tribal domestic architecture can be seen only in southern Florida. Here the Seminole and Miccosukee frame their traditional houses — known as *chickee* — with peeled cypress, roof them with deep eaves of palmetto leaves for maximum shade and deck them with boards to protect workers and sleepers from snakes and periodic flooding. Four or five *chickees* for sleeping and working are grouped around a central open-eave cooking *chickee* with its characteristic star-shaped fire. The camps consist of kin related through the maternal line and can be seen along the Tamiami Trail as well as in the Everglades on silt islands known as hammocks.

Great Plains–Plateau

Spanish first entering the southern Plains saw painted,
portable hide-covered tents — mainstays for seminomadic
hunters who followed the buffalo. Now popularly known
by the Sioux word *tipi,* meaning "to dwell," the lodges
could be easily dismantled, their short poles and bundled
covers carried by dogs. But not only hunters occupied the
grasslands that extended from the Mexican border to
Canada and lay between the Mississippi River and the
Rockies. Along river valleys in the central and northern
Plains, farming tribes began building large earth lodges by
the ninth century. Framed of cottonwood, roofed with
sticks and grasses and topped with sod or loose earth, these
structures were originally rectangular in plan. Possibly the
central Plains peoples, such as the Pawnee, introduced the
circular form that predominated by the 14th century.

By the late 18th century the Mandan and Hidatsa tribes
were consolidating their earth lodges into stockaded large
villages along the upper Missouri River. Social rules
governed construction: The men erected the four heavy
central posts, rafters and side walls, while the women, as in
most Native American cultures considered the owners and
custodians of domestic space, completed the earthen covering and furnished the large dwellings. Inside would be a
sweat bath for cleansing and purification and excavated
storage cellars or caches for dried corn and beans; after the
tribes acquired houses from the Spanish, favored mounts
would be picketed within as well. Occupants slept in
screened booths around the slanting side wall. These

Opposite: Mat-covered tipi of the Umatilla tribe, about 1900. (Lee Moorhouse, Smithsonian Institution National Anthropological Archives)

Below: Kickulie pit house, the oldest plateau house type. (American Museum of Natural History)

summer villages near the floodplain gardens were considered home; the other seasons were spent in tents on the hunt or in small earth lodges protected by tree cover.

Smaller earth-covered homes, known popularly as pit houses, were used in the plateau region between the upper Plains and the Northwest Coast. Their round floors, rarely more than 20 feet in diameter, were excavated as deep as three feet. Unlike the regular Plains earth lodge with its prominent tunnel entryway, these were entered by a notched-log ladder through the smoke hole. The plateau also featured multifamily houses framed of stout poles, in profile resembling the Great Lakes extended conical *wigwam* except that they were roofed with reed mats instead of birch bark.

A unique Plains structure used by southern tribes such as the Wichita was the grass house. Framed of split red cedar ribs bent over an interior support ring of cottonwood posts, it had a grass thatched covering twisted at the peak to form a distinctive steeple, with four of the ribs —representing the sacred four directions — piercing the roof.

As the Spanish horses proliferated throughout the Plains in the 17th century, nomadic architecture became refined. With mounts to transport poles and heavy buffalo-hide covers, *tipis* doubled in size. Now tribes could take advantage of the full strength and length of lodgepole pine; their covers could now use more than 20, rather than six to eight, buffalo hides, expertly tanned, sewn and smoked by craftswomen's guilds. The southern Plains Kiowa and northern Blackfeet became renowned for their painted *tipi* covers, which depicted either battle exploits or supernatural guardians envisioned during four-day fasts. Such designs were handed down through families.

One Plains structure that is now found throughout Native America is the *wigwam*-framed sweat bath. Covered with tarps or quilts, the little dome contains a pit for rocks heated cherry-red in a nearby fire. As celebrants ladle water to create stinging steam, prayers are spoken. Almost as widespread is the use of canvas *tipis* at powwow gatherings and for religious ceremonies of the Native American Church, which uses peyote, the hallucinogenic cactus, as its sacrament.

Wichita reservation seen about 1900 and containing many building types — grass thatched houses, summer arbors (covered only on top), log cabins and tents. (Western History Collections, University of Oklahoma Library)

Wichita grass house. (Bob Easton)

Pawnee earth lodge, village on the Loup Fork, Neb., about 1871. The interior structure was made of cottonwood, while the skin was built with willow sapling rafters, grass and sod. (William H. Jackson, National Anthropological Archives)

Crow camp on the Little Big Horn River. With the greater mobility allowed by the horse, the architecture of Plains tribes changed. (Montana Historical Society)

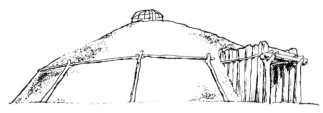

Opposite and above: Hidatsa earth lodges. Woven grass matting was tied over closely placed willow sapling rafters. Sod packed over the grass completed the structure. (Bob Easton)

Southwest

Three prehistoric architectural traditions once existed in the arid deserts, mesa lands and pine-covered mountains between the Colorado and Rio Grande rivers and into the Colorado plateau. Centered in southern Arizona, Mogollon culture was notable for the structural variety of its rectangular and circular pit houses. Situated nearer the Gila River, Hohokam society experienced steady development for thousands of years, reaching its technological peak with canals that ran for hundreds of miles and thick-walled multistory citadels, notably the Casa Grande.

Best-known are the ruins of Anasazi settlements, which are concentrated in the Four Corners region in the north and Chaco Canyon in the south. The Anasazi are famous for their honeycombed room clusters and circular *kivas* (social-ceremonial chambers). In sites along the Colorado plateau such as Mesa Verde, their towns are commonly nestled beneath south-facing overhanging sandstone cliffs. In the Chaco region they are compacted into defensible small kivas, a centrally located great kiva and room units that extend to five stories and open onto roof terraces where people spent much of their workday.

The pre-Columbian period also saw Athabaskan-speaking immigrants from the Canadian northwest enter the Southwest with an entirely different architectural attitude. Known today as the Apache and Navajo, they introduced distinctive single-family house forms — the Navajo *hogan* and the Apache *wikiup.* Although Navajos in particular adopted much of the symbolism and technology of the pre-existing Pueblos (descendants of the Mogollon and Anasazi), they resisted aggregating their houses, preferring dispersed extended-family homesteads.

The older hogan style, the so-called forked-stick or male hogan, was essentially an adobe pyramid with an extended doorway. The later hogan, the female hogan, originally used a corbeled-log roof either built up from ground level and covered with earth or placed atop rock, log, railroad ties or even concrete block walls. Playing prominent roles in Navajo mythology and ritual, hogans always face east and are consecrated in rituals that unite them with cosmic prototypes.

Opposite: Walpi Pueblo, First Mesa, Ariz. Strategically perched on a mesa top, Walpi has been occupied by the Hopi for hundreds of years. (Los Angeles County Museum of Natural History)

Cliff dwellings at Mesa Verde, Colo., inhabited by the Anasazi until about A.D. 1275. These provided defensible settlements as well as climatic protection. Underground *kivas* marked clan "neighborhoods."

Navajo hogan of stacked logs. This typically six-sided hogan has notched-log walls and a corbeled-log roof. (Arizona State Museum, University of Arizona)

Stone *kiva*, Puye, N.M., seen about 1920. (T. Harmon Parkhurst, Museum of New Mexico)

Zuni Pueblo, Zuni, N.M., in 1880. Thought to be one of the Seven Cities of Cibola, it was first "discovered" by Coronado's expedition in 1539. (Southwest Museum, Los Angeles)

Interior, Zuni Pueblo, about 1899. Interiors were often beautifully painted, their designs lighted by skylights and their space filled with little more than a low ledge for a shelf or seat. (Los Angeles Museum of Natural History)

Papago house. (Bob Easton)

Taos Pueblo, Taos, N.M., in 1880. The north block rises five stories above the plaza. Buildings could be defended by pulling up the ground-floor ladders. (Museum of New Mexico)

The river-dwelling Pima and desert-foraging Papago were Hohokam descendants. By historic times they were also inhabiting single-family structures, the mud-roofed *ki,* lower than the hogan with a four-post interior frame. Mexican influence saw these older structures soon forsaken in favor of rectangular adobe houses with large attached arbors. However, the *ki* superstructure is preserved today in the Papago rainhouse with its special *wato* arbor, ritual structures used exclusively for their annual cactus wine festival.

After the 13th century the Anasazi and Mogollon descendants formed numerous city-states called *pueblos* by the early Spanish. Commonly grouped as the eastern or Rio Grande River *pueblos* and the western *pueblos* (the Hopi and Zuni), *pueblo* town plans are often architecturally distinguished as plaza and parallel street types. Street-type *pueblos,* such as Acoma, N.M., and Santo Domingo, N.M., are generally made up of blocks of multistory houses with set-back terraces facing south to maximize the heat-sink properties of adobe: Their walls absorb the day's sunlight, so that at night the heat radiates within. With the additional warmth from small, wood-burning fireplaces, occupants sleep comfortably even in midwinter. Plaza-type *pueblos* are arrayed around centrally located ceremonial arenas. Roof terraces were much-used working and socializing spaces, with sleeping rooms facing them and storage chambers deeper within the house block holding great quantities of dried food.

Many *pueblos* still exist in Arizona and New Mexico today. Although Anglo building materials such as window glass, windows, doors, stovepipes and cement have altered their construction, communities such as Taos, N.M., Walpi, Ariz., and Acoma, N.M., retain significant traditional appearance for visitors and great cultural importance to their native owners.

California

In California, between the Sierra Mountains and the Pacific Ocean, Native American buildings reflect a variety of habitats. In the north a constellation of tribes arranged their wood plank houses in hamlets (in California generally termed *rancherias*) where the Trinity and Klamath rivers pour into the ocean. For family houses they built three-pitch structures of thick, unfinished planks split with elkhorn wedges and stone mauls from cedar (preferred by the Hupa) or redwood (the Yurok choice). Residents slept using wooden pillows and stools in shoulder-high, plank-reinforced pits warmed by a central hearth.

The second northern building, a men's two-pitch sweat house, which often featured an overturned dugout canoe on the ridge to keep out rain, was more deeply excavated. Both buildings were entered through circular doorways, but the exit from the sweat house was through a roof opening onto a south-facing sun deck built of river boulders. Periodic reconstruction of these sweat houses was a sacred activity with world renewal or fishing season ritualism.

In the damp, temperate central California climate, Native Americans built with materials at hand. Near the coast, simple thatched domical lodges — both single-family buildings sometimes arranged in semicircular camps and extended domical multifamily houses, such as those thatched with tules by the lake-dwelling Pomo — sufficed to stave off rains and fogs. For ceremonies, large earth-covered round houses were built. Along the central valley trough, however, small pit houses similar to the plateau houses were clustered around larger ceremonial earth lodges. In the Sierra foothills, the Miwok and Maidu leaned large redwood bark slabs against conical pole frames for cozier protection against snowfall and wind.

In the drier, hotter south, architecture was more ephemeral. The Chumash used high, grass-thatched buildings featuring such amenities as limpet-shell "doorbells." Nearer the Mexican border religious gatherings called for open-air arenas entirely surrounded by brush arbors. Native dwellings here fell under Mexican peasant influence with *rancherias* near old Catholic missions containing gabled, thatched structures, walled with adobe bricks or upright posts or cactus stalks, or using the sandwich technique of staggered horizontal lattice between corner posts with thick adobe filling the interstices.

Miwok round house, Calavaras County, in 1901, with a high entrance roof. Round houses had pole frames and were roofed and sided with split planks. (Hartman, Peabody Museum, Harvard University)

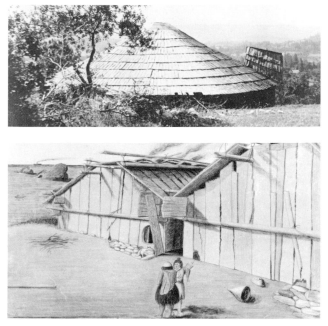

Plank houses, Trinidad Bay, Calif., drawn by J. G. Buff in 1850. (Henry E. Huntington Library and Art Gallery)

The Yuman-speaking peoples who tilled the Colorado River floodplain each spring built sand-roofed houses, framed with heavy mesquite, which backed into the river shore terrace and featured flat fronts with granaries on stilts atop or beside them.

Under Anglo influence the traditional earthen dance houses of the central area were transformed into wood-shingled round houses. In isolated native settlements today, however, such buildings are still used for ceremonies; some are built entirely of wood, others with a sunken earth-lodge base combined with a shake roof.

Yokuts arbor-shaded village of typical brush materials. (Stephen Powers, *Tribes of California*)

Brush houses of a Paiute tribe, northern Arizona, in 1873. (John K. Hillers, Smithsonian Institution)

Tlingit chief's house, Cape Fox Village, Alaska, in 1899. The painted exterior has a bear motif. (National Anthropological Archives)

Arctic–Northwest Coast

The Alaskan Arctic is the westernmost corner of a 5,000-mile cultural region inhabited by many Eskimo groups whose architecture was almost uniformly divided between summer and winter dwellings. For the freezing months single families — sometimes one man with two wives — occupied sod-insulated, semisubterranean buildings with long, downward-sloping tunnel entryways and raised sleeping decks in the rear. These features allowed exploitation of every degree of heat from human bodies and oil-burning soapstone lamps. The famous snow-block house was generally not found here, since there was ample sod and driftwood for more permanently framing the winter house.

Summer saw people exchanging their cavelike winter houses for *tupik* (summer tents), which were pitched at coastal or riverside locations where they fished, berried and embarked on whaling expeditions. In the western Arctic was developed the *kasim,* a social-ceremonial men's retreat for storytelling, communal dancing, sweating and socializing. *Kasims* were in essence expanded versions of the regular winter house; some could shelter a hundred guests.

The south Alaskan peninsula is home to one tribe, the Tlingit, that partakes of the great Northwest Coast architectural heritage. Although most of the Northwest Coast peoples — tribes such as the Haida, Kwakiutl and Tsimshian — live under Canadian jurisdiction, the Tlingit country is part of the United States. Occupying villages protected by tree-lined bays and beaches facing the Pacific Ocean, the Tlingit built massive gabled-roof houses framed

Opposite: Tlingit house interior, Klukwan, Alaska, about 1895. Interior screens were carved and painted on cedar planks and set up for winter ceremonials. (American Museum of Natural History)

Interior of a Salish winter lodge, a typical wood shed-roof house, as painted by Paul Kane in 1850. (National Gallery of Canada, Ottawa)

Eskimo skin tent house and whalebone fireplace, Plover Bay, Alaska, in 1899. (Museum of the American Indian, Heye Foundation)

with adzed cedar posts and sheathed with mortised hand-split cedar planks and large-shake roofs. Arranged in a curving line, the buildings conformed to the inlet's shoreline, facing the beached canoes. House interiors reflected social division: Slaves slept around the large rectangular fire pit on the polished wood floor, commoners occupied the next rectangular tier, and noble families enjoyed separate cubicles on the uppermost tier.

In sculpted frontal poles, sculpted interior posts and painted house screens, Tlingit houses displayed crests and mythological imagery evoking the wealth and prestige of their occupants, all of whom belonged to the same lineage. During the winter, the sacred season, these images sprang to life during elaborate performances for which the house was transformed into a ceremonial stage. During the summer, the secular season, the coastal village would be emptied as tribes moved upstream to family-owned hunting, fishing and foraging spots.

Along the upper Oregon and Washington coasts, shed-roofed structures of cedar planks split with wedges and mauls were constructed by Salish-speaking tribes. Social hierarchy gave way to greater egalitarianism here, reflected in the fact that entire tribes might sleep and eat under one roof, which could extend for 500 feet or more along the waterfront. On all sides would be curtain walls, horizontal planks lashed between pole uprights. For gift-giving feasts known throughout the Northwest Coast as potlatches, special houses might be built as warehouses or for the ceremonial exchange of large amounts of blankets and vessels. ▨

NATIVE HAWAIIANS
Ray Morris

The roots of Hawaiian architecture probably lie in the South Pacific, near Australia and New Guinea. A series of migrations north and east over the centuries led to the colonization of Hawaii by settlers from the Marquesas about A.D. 300. According to archeologists, these first settlers may have built pole-and-thatch dwellings with pebble floors very much like houses Hawaiians erected in the 18th and 19th centuries. Although indigenous buildings were constructed well into the 19th century, no genuine examples survive. However, accounts written since the arrival of Captain James Cook in 1778 as well as one reconstructed house, created for the Bishop Museum in 1902 from parts of three originals, provide a glimpse of native architectural practices.

Hawaiians built using adzes of a hard, flintlike stone found near volcanic craters and sometimes made with a wooden handle. In addition, they worked with knives formed from pieces of shark jawbone embedded in wooden handles.

Some houses were created by bending together adjacent trees to form the frame. More often, trees cut in the mountains were arranged in a frame consisting of major and minor ridge poles supported by vertical posts. Both the bent-tree and framed houses contained *pou-hana* (vertical posts running from ground to ridge at the center of each gable end). Flanking the *pou-hana* in the framed houses were shorter posts, called *kukuna* (rays), that supported the end rafters. Additional posts spaced evenly along the side walls, and sometimes wall plates, supported the ends of the rafters. The posts were inserted in the earth if possible and steadied as necessary by a stone plinth projecting above the surface. The parts of the frame were connected with carved joints and lashed with *sennit*. This was a cord women made by rolling the inner bark of the olona plant or strands of uki uki grass between their palms and thighs, then braiding

Grass houses in the village of Makakupa in Ka'ū District on the island of Hawaii, as depicted by Thomas Heddington after a visit by Captain George Vancouver in 1792 – 94. (Bishop Museum)

three strands of the resulting fiber to produce the finished product.

The completed frame was covered with *aho* (small horizontal sticks to which bundles of thatch were tied). Pili grass was preferred for this covering, but other grasses, as well as leaves of ti, sugar cane and hala, were also used. The ridge was protected with banana plant sheaths.

The construction of a house had religious as well as utilitarian significance. The *pou-hana*, for example, were thought to possess supernatural powers, and at their erection the house was said to pass from ideal to real existence. The thatch above the doors of important Hawaiians' houses was left untrimmed until the building was ready to be occupied. Then a *kahuna* (priest) offered a lengthy prayer and trimmed the last bit of thatch, a ceremony referred to as cutting the umbilical cord of the house.

Some Hawaiian settlements were quite large. Captain Cook described Kailua at Kona, Hawaii, as a village of 700 or 800 dwellings. Within it, the houses were all built in the thatched house tradition, but they differed greatly in appearance, size and quality. The gabled and hipped roofs varied in pitch; no house was to be higher than that of the local *ali'i* (chief). While Cook noted some buildings 20 to 30 feet wide and 40 to 50 feet long, most were "mere hovels . . ., not unlike oblong corn or hay stacks," with their entrances "made indifferently, in the end or side." Ordinarily Hawaiians typically owned one house of this sort. Archeological remains at Kailua include those of houses as small as 6 by 8 feet, which probably stood 4 to 5 feet high. These served mainly for storage and shelter from occasional inclement weather; otherwise, most daily activities took place outdoors. In one corner, a pile of mats and tapa cloth made a sleeping place while, according to Cook, a bench at one end served as a storage place for household

Hawaiian chiefs meeting with the captain and officers of the frigate *Vénus* in a large thatched structure, from an 1837 lithograph by Louis-Jules Masselot. (Bishop Museum)

Hawaiian village of the 1820 period, re-created in Hilo by the author in 1956 but destroyed by a 1960 tidal wave. This chief's compound contained (from left to right) a canoe shed, storage house, cook's house, women's workshop, women's meeting house, family house and men's meeting house. (Ray Morris)

Traditional Hawaiian grass house (pre-1900). After the frame was made, small sticks were attached to cover the exterior, and thatch was lashed to this framework. (Bishop Museum)

Framing of a Hawaiian thatched house standing on a stone platform. The lack of diagonal bracing caused the frame to sag eventually and gave the house its characteristic "tumbled" look. (Ray Morris)

Robert Louis Stevenson's grass hut at the Waioli Tea House, Manoa, in 1939. Thatching usually was started at the bottom and proceeded upward. (Bishop Museum)

Sennit braid used to lash the frames of Hawaiian houses. *Sennit* made of olona fiber was so strong that the Hawaiians continued to use it long after rope was available. (Ray Morris)

Hawaiian family in front of their thatched house. The ridge thatching required expert craftsmanship to make the roof rainproof. (Bishop Museum)

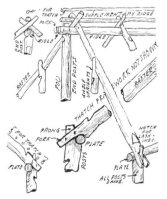

Framing techniques used in early Hawaiian grass houses, as recorded by David Malo. Shown are carpentry details of the ridge, rafters and posts, including the unusual way in which the rafters and posts were positioned with a spikelike tenon protruding upward through a forked mortise on the lower end of the rafter. (Ray Morris)

utensils. Even these were not the lowliest dwellings. The poorest people sometimes lived in holes in the ground, cliffs, caves or open sheds.

High-ranking Hawaiians, on the other hand, owned several well-built and well-furnished houses. Many were set on 12-to-18-inch-high floor platforms, covered with sand and rendered more comfortable by a covering of mats composed of *lauhala* (the leaf of the pandanus plant). According to 19th-century accounts, six separate buildings made up an ideal *kauhale* (household cluster) of an *ali'i: hale noa*, where the family slept; *hale kua*, where the women worked; *hale aina*, the women's eating house; the *mua*, forbidden to women, in which men ate and offered daily worship to ancestral deities; *hale pe'a*, a house for quarantining menstruating women; and *heiau*, a house for worship. Some Hawaiians also owned a *halau* (canoe house), *hale kāhumu* (oven shed) and *hale papa'a*, for storing crops and agricultural tools. Others fitted their houses with an *aleo* (storage loft).

The coming of Europeans and Asians brought changes to Hawaiian traditions and finally eradicated them entirely. David Malo, a Hawaiian who wrote a mid-19th-century account of traditional life in Hawaii, recorded that the use of mortar to cement the house foundations became popular among native builders after the missionaries began to arrive in the early 1820s. Then, he said, wood houses covered with boards, adobe houses and "houses made of cloth," all introduced by outsiders, supplanted traditional forms altogether. Nevertheless, the continued preference for one-story houses in Hawaii may grow out of memories of the thatched house tradition. In the 20th century, interest in island history has led some scholars to excavate Hawaiian archeological sites and to attempt reconstruction of native houses. In addition, Hawaiian architects have introduced mixtures of Asian and Hawaiian forms into their designs for resorts and other new buildings as more explicit references to the islands' traditional architecture. ▨

Ralph Fitkin House (1937, Ray Morris), on the slopes of Diamond Head, Honolulu, a contemporary house using a Hawaiian-style roof and other details reflecting island traditions. (Ray Morris)

Gable-end entry, rectangular
house in Angola, an antecedent of
the shotgun house. *(Angola and
the River Congo,* 1876)

Right: Two-room house of the
Yoruba people, Ilefunfun, Nigeria.
(John Michael Vlach)

Rural Haitian house type used as
slave quarters in the 18th century.
(John Michael Vlach)

AFRO-AMERICANS
John Michael Vlach

The first Africans to settle permanently in the United States were purchased as slaves at Jamestown, Va., in 1619, a full year before the arrival of the Pilgrims at Plymouth, Mass. Since then, African-based traditions have helped shape American expressive culture — speech patterns, oral literature, music, popular dances and foods, as well as material culture, although black folk architecture in the United States remains, for the most part, a hidden heritage.

Beyond negative public attitudes toward black people arising from a national history of slavery and racism, the denial of this architectural contribution has much to do with the fact that African and European folk housing is similar in several basic ways: The two building traditions share a repertoire of plans, methods of construction and a preference for certain building materials. A free-standing, one-story, rectangular house of two or three rooms with mud walls and a thatched roof could just as easily have been found in England or Ireland as in what is now Ghana or Nigeria. The cabins of slaves and white yeoman farmers found first along the southeastern Atlantic coast and later in the frontier back country were so similar that it is often difficult to assign cultural origins. Only rigorous histories of particular times and places can reveal the specific traditions or the degree of cultural synthesis that occurred.

The single- and double-pen cabins common to the lowland South, structures of one or two rooms, are as African in plan as they are European. However, their typical scale as well as their usual modes of construction give them a decided Euro-American character. Nevertheless, neither African-based techniques for using vegetal materials nor a preference for small, intimate spaces vanished completely. Some slaves in Georgia are known to have built small houses with wickerwork walls of woven branches plastered with mud, and one such building in South Carolina survived into the early 20th century. The thatched roofs on outbuildings known as "critter houses" built by some South Carolina blacks as late as the 1930s were a response not only to their poverty but also to their memory of older African practices.

Although most of the efforts of Afro-American carpenters have blended anonymously into the regional landscape of the South, one building type stands out — the shotgun house. This house type is one room wide, one story tall and several rooms deep (usually three or more) and has its primary entrance in the gable end. Its perpendicular alignment breaks with the usual Euro-American pattern, in which the gables are on the sides and the entrance is on the facade or long side. Although gable-entry houses occur in some parts of central Africa, the shotgun house is a New World hybrid that developed in the West Indies and entered the United States via New Orleans in the early 19th century. American shotgun houses derive from the fusion of distinct ethnic architectural components: a Caribbean Indian building shape, European colonial framing techniques and African-inspired proxemic codes. In the United States they should be understood as the contribution of the free people of color from Haiti. Thus, the roots of Afro-

Opposite: **Contemporary urban house in Ile-Ife, Nigeria, showing a broad front porch resembling a veranda. (John Michael Vlach)**

Above and right: House near Edgefield, S.C., built by an ex-slave from the Congo region. The frame structure has walls made of lath lashed in place and covered on the inside with grass, as well as a grass thatched roof. (Charles J. Montgomery, *American Anthropologist.* 1908)

Two-room frame house near Beaufort, S.C., with a porch, mud-and-stick chimney and shed addition in 1938. (Marion Post Wolcott, FSA, Library of Congress)

American architecture are to be found not only in mother Africa but also in the Caribbean.

Shotgun houses are particularly prominent in New Orleans, but they can be found throughout the South, where they are used as farmhouses for tenants, as rental houses in towns and as workers' houses in mill and mining towns, lumber camps, oil fields and railroad yards. The suitability of this building type to all these contexts encouraged widespread adoption, so that its present distribution reaches from the Carolinas to California and from the Gulf Coast to the south side of Chicago. Shotgun houses continue to be associated primarily with black populations and may be considered an expression of ethnic architecture despite their national diffusion and the fact that in some communities many whites live in them too.

More ubiquitous than the shotgun house is the front porch, which may be tallied as an African-derived trait. No antecedent for the front porch, as it is commonly found in the South, can be found in England or elsewhere in northern Europe. The experience of tropical heat and humidity inspired such additions, and verandas are common to African house design. Soon after both slaves and their masters arrived in the New World, a cross-cultural encounter occurred, and generations of white builders adopted the custom of porch building. Although the Victorian period spawned galleries and verandas on houses all over the United States, for almost 250 years the southern front porch has owed its existence mainly to the adaptive genius of local carpenters acting on African notions of good architectural form. ▨

Right: Plan of a shotgun house,
Port-au-Prince, Haiti, built with
front and side porches. (John
Michael Vlach)

Far right: Plan of a shotgun house,
New Orleans. A bathroom was
added to the third room in this
century. (John Michael Vlach)

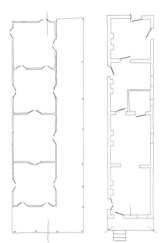

Urban shotgun house with a
double entrance, Port-au-Prince,
Haiti. (John Michael Vlach)

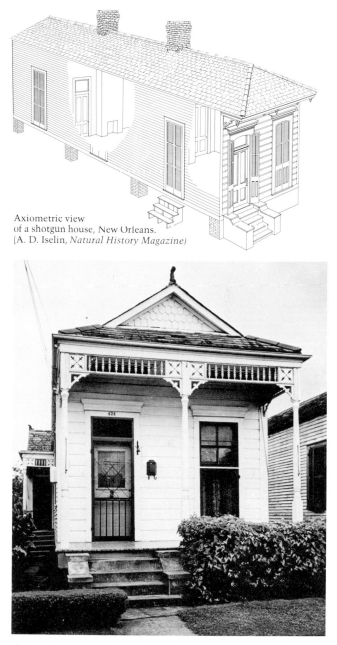

Axiometric view
of a shotgun house, New Orleans.
(A. D. Iselin, *Natural History Magazine*)

Shotgun house with Carpenter Gothic ornamentation, New Orleans.
(Elemore Morgan, Historic New Orleans Collection)

Opposite: Shotgun house along
Bayou LaFourche, La., the home of
a sugarcane worker in 1937.
(Dorothea Lange, FSA, Library
of Congress)

DUTCH
Dell Upton

New World Dutch architecture presents two paradoxes: First, colonial "Dutch" architecture, incorporating Netherlandish traditions, particularly structural systems, was built by people of many ethnic origins, ranging from African to Scandinavian. Second, except for a few buildings dubiously attributed to the 17th century, all surviving Dutch buildings were constructed betwen the early 18th and 19th centuries, long after Dutch rule ended. The continuation of Dutch architectural traditions attests to the remarkable architectural conservatism of the non-English population and the relative lack of English settlement in Dutch areas until late in the colonial era.

These colonial Dutch buildings were the products of the first of two distinct migrations from the Low Countries to North America. Their builders came to the Dutch West India Company's colony of New Netherland, which stretched from the Connecticut River to the Delaware River, with settlement concentrated in the Hudson River Valley of present-day New York and New Jersey. Most of the settlers arrived between 1614 and 1664, when the English captured New Netherland; by 1664 about 8,000 people, not all of them Dutch, lived in New Netherland. A second wave of immigrants — nearly 200,000 — settled between 1840 and 1910 in a broad band of the upper Midwest stretching from Michigan to Iowa. Although they created a recognizable landscape, it has never been closely studied.

The colonial settlers' most durable contribution to New World Dutch architecture was a framing system distinguished by parallel H-shaped bents or transverse frames. These ran the short way across a building — front to back in a house — and consisted of square vertical posts linked by horizontal beams called *ankerbalken* (anchorbeams), enormous timbers 12 to 15 inches deep that were set a third to halfway down the tops of the posts. The anchorbeams were often supported at the ends by *korbeels* (diagonal braces or curved knee braces). Larger buildings were constructed by adding aisles to one or both long sides of the basic frame,

Opposite: Verplanck House, Fishkill-on-the-Hudson, N.Y. Its "Dutch" roof may have been a British innovation.

Desmarest-Gurd House (c. 1681), New Milford, N.J., a "Flemish" Dutch house, in 1936. The stucco has since been removed. (HABS)

Samuel Desmarest House (c. 1679), New Milford, N.J., a common type of New World Dutch rural house built with an even number of openings. (HABS)

Johannes Luyster House (1717 – 18), Holland, N.J., whose symmetrical facade is shaded by wide overhanging eaves. (HABS)

creating a basilican structure. Anchorbeam bents gave the exterior of the Dutch building its distinctive chunky proportions. Painted red to contrast with whitewashed walls, *ankerbalken* defined the Dutch interior visually. The heart of New World Dutch building, they represented solidity and prosperity, especially when compared to those used in Holland.

Dutch builders also used limestone, sandstone and brick, but these were late 17th-century additions to the repertoire, and the *ankerbalken* remained important. Many brick buildings contained complete load-bearing timber frames; the brick was a veneer and occasionally was not even applied to all four sides of the structure. Dutch masonry builders liked to decorate the exteriors of their

Foster-Armstrong House (c. 1790s), Montague, N.J., a gambrel-roof frame house with a stone addition constructed after 1812. Built as a public house, the original portion is more characteristic of coastal Dutch architecture than the upper Delaware Valley. (George Eisenman, HABS)

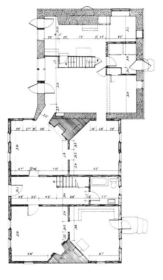

Right: First-floor plan of the Foster-Armstrong House, showing the center hall and the relationship of the two sections of the house. (John Albers, HABS)

A reunion at the Foster-Armstrong House, when a second-floor balcony had been added. (HABS Collection)

Front elevation of the house. (Gary Kreger, HABS)

structures. Initials, dates and patterns were picked out in black glazed bricks against a surface made lively by stepped joints of cross-band brickwork and finished at the edges by parapets that were sometimes stepped.

Unlike most colonial ethnic populations, the Dutch came from a heavily urban society and thought of themselves as city people and traders above all. Dutch settlement in the 17th and early 18th centuries clustered around two principal urban centers — New Amsterdam (now New York City) and Fort Orange or Beverwyck (now Albany, N.Y.) — and a smaller village, Wiltwyck (now Kingston, N.Y.), about halfway between them. Town authorities strove to legislate true urbanity. They required that substantial, permanently inhabited houses be constructed, that corner lots be built up first to achieve an appearance of urban density and that vacant lots be confiscated and resold to purchasers who would build. Dutch city dwellers built one- and two-room houses, one or two stories tall, set gable end to the street. City regulations required that the street front gables be veneered with brick for fire protection, but the wooden cladding was often left exposed on the other sides. Individual Dutch buildings survived in New York City until after the American Revolution. Albany retained its Dutch appearance into the early 19th century, and specimens of Dutch architecture survived until the early 20th century.

The Dutch also introduced a number of distinctive rural building types. Many prosperous early builders constructed Netherlandish house-barns, aisled structures up to 120 feet long. A house-barn combined under a single roof a dwelling for the farmer, living quarters for farm workers, storage areas for crops and space for animals.

Although the freestanding Dutch barn is sometimes described as a New World invention created by separating the living and farm spaces of a house-barn, examples have been recorded in Europe. As constructed here from the late 17th to the early 19th centuries, the Dutch barn was an aisled anchorbeam structure three or four bays long, entered from the gable end. The central area, defined by the main bents, contained a threshing floor at ground level and hay storage on movable poles laid across the *ankerbalken.* One side aisle housed cattle and the other horses; each aisle was entered through its own gable-end door. Above the stalls were additional crop storage spaces.

A third Dutch farm building, constructed in northern New Jersey into the 20th century, was the hay barracks, an open-sided structure used to shelter hay stacks. A hay barracks consisted of four or five poles supporting a pyramidal or gabled roof that could be moved up or down with levers, according to the size of the stack under them.

Regional and ethnic variations in Dutch houses make a simple or comprehensive description impossible. The commonest New World Dutch rural house was a one- or two-room nucleus of a sort indigenous to most western European rural people. Most had an even number of openings on their long walls, and many had a front door into each room but no rear doors. Gabled roofs were standard; the "Dutch" gambrel roof was a mid-18th-century innovation probably brought to the American colonies by English builders. On the interior, a jambless fireplace, an enormous brick hearth with its chimney hood suspended from the ceiling to carry off smoke but with no side walls, was a distinctive feature.

Abraham Yates House (mid-18th century), Schenectady, N.Y., the only surviving Dutch urban house. (Jack E. Boucher, HABS)

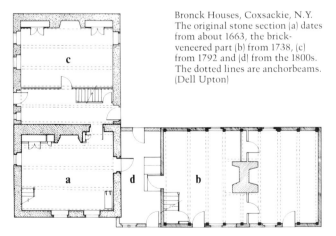

Bronck Houses, Coxsackie, N.Y. The original stone section (a) dates from about 1663, the brick-veneered part (b) from 1738, (c) from 1792 and (d) from the 1800s. The dotted lines are anchorbeams. (Dell Upton)

Like other 18th-century Americans, Dutch builders responded to international popular culture by introducing central passages and double-pile, or two-room-deep, plans to their houses. Often, too, they abandoned the even-bay facade for a symmetrical three- or five-bay facade. Dutch barns were built later than Dutch houses, and the Dutch framing system can be found in rural buildings dating from the 1830s.

In the 50 years after the American Revolution, as Dutch strongholds were penetrated by Anglo-American popula-

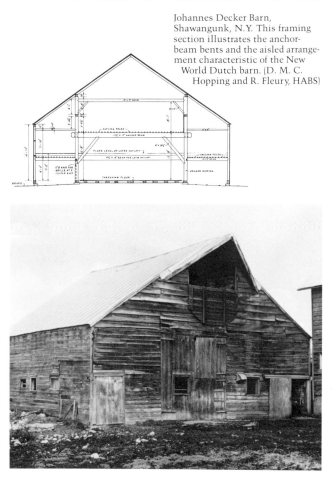

Johannes Decker Barn, Shawangunk, N.Y. This framing section illustrates the anchorbeam bents and the aisled arrangement characteristic of the New World Dutch barn. (D. M. C. Hopping and R. Fleury, HABS)

Dutch barn, Richmond Hill, N.Y. The openings have been altered, but the original pattern of a large central door with smaller doors at either side survives. (Dell Upton)

Van Hoesen House (c. 1730), Columbia County, N.Y., showing a corbel supporting the anchorbeam. (Dell Upton)

tions and popular architectural ideas, Dutch ethnic plans and decoration ceased to be used. Yet, Dutch architectural traditions were not simply abandoned; they were modified and rechanneled. Even where Netherlandish features could no longer be found, ethnic ties and preferences remained. For example, after the anchorbeam bent was abandoned in the 19th century, the chunky story-and-a-half proportions that it engendered survived as a visual preference among rural home builders for another half century. ▨

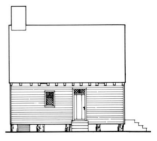

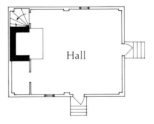

Planter's house reconstructed at St. Mary's City, Md. Such small, one-room structures, raised quickly and covered economically with split oak or chestnut clapboards, were common in the 17th-century Tidewater but have all disappeared. (Colonial Williamsburg Foundation)

Right: Elevation and plan of the Woodward-Jones House (1716), Nansemond County, Va., one of the oldest surviving frame dwellings in the Tidewater South. (Cary Carson)

Fairbanks House (c. 1637; additions, 17th and 18th centuries), Dedham, Mass., the oldest standing structure in English North America. The house, since restored, epitomizes New Englanders' improved standard of living. (SPNEA)

Hall

ENGLISH
Cary Carson

Once upon a time thoroughbred descendants of English immigrants in North America understood "ethnic groups" to mean everybody else and "ethnic culture" to be an oxymoron. Thomas Jefferson was neither the first nor the last to belittle "whatever is not English among us." English laws, English language, English goods and, above all, English swagger were the carrots and sticks that the ruling culture used to Anglicize newcomers from Germany, Switzerland, Holland, Ireland, Scandinavia and Africa, as well as the native peoples whom the English displaced and dispossessed. Their success, however, was not complete. Foreign customs proved surprisingly hardy among immigrant groups. Moreover, British traditions themselves were succumbing to outside influences well before the end of the 18th century, even in the mother country. England's contribution to the genealogy of American architecture was therefore less pure blooded — and makes a more interesting story — than many of her progeny have assumed.

At first all English domestic building in the colonies was vernacular building, conceived and executed according to such local customs as immigrants remembered from home. Their new circumstances forced several choices. Often the first was a decision to build a house and barns as cheaply as possible to save limited capital for land, labor and livestock. New arrivals in all colonies and homesteaders on each new frontier employed a variety of Old World building technologies to erect inexpensive, impermanent structures sufficient for "ordinary beginners." When farms and plantations later prospered, such earth-walled, log and post-in-the-ground buildings were replaced by elaborately carpentered "great or English framed" houses full of expensively hewn timbers, sawn boards and intricate joinery. This homesteading sequence was soon completed in socially stable and agriculturally diversified New England, where many early dwellings still survive. It was harder for southern planters to accumulate and pass on wealth in the unhealthy one-crop Chesapeake colonies, which remained perpetual frontiers with few durable buildings until after 1700.

The arrangement of living and working space inside the earliest dwellings followed many different regional English practices at first because colonists initially were reluctant to give up familiar habits of household life. Eventually they learned that certain imported house types and farmsteads were more suitable than others. New Englanders — those not confined to very small houses — came to prefer a lowland English plan that gave nuclear families access to an all-purpose hall, a parlor for sleeping and entertaining and a lean-to kitchen on the ground floor, work rooms and additional sleeping chambers on the floor above, and attics and cellars for storage and food preservation. Immigrants from mixed farming regions in Great Britain combined crop storage and cow stalls into an innovative dual-purpose barn, which joined granaries, stables and pig sties to make a typical New England farmyard.

Virginians and Marylanders chose differently. Many lived in flimsy, cheaply built one- and two-room houses. Wealthier planters found that an English west country plan divided a one-story house conveniently into halves — a hall, inner room and attic chambers for a master's family and a

Parson Capen House (1683), Tops-
field, Mass., built in a typical hall
and parlor plan with bedrooms and
attics above. (Cary Carson)

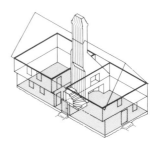

Cushing Barn (c. 1679; c. 1693 –
1700), Hingham, Mass. A porch
entry for carts and a threshing
floor separated calf pens from cow
stalls. Hay and straw were stored
in lofts. (Robert St. George)

Mathews Manor (c. 1650), War-
wick County, Va., a familiar
English plan providing an inner
room, heated hall, passage and
service room. (Cary Carson)

Burrage's End tobacco barn (18th century), Anne Arundel County, Md.,
framed with lapped and nailed joints. Tobacco barns were partitioned into
bays the length of the drying racks. (Colonial Williamsburg Foundation)

separate work room or kitchen with quarters overhead for indentured servants and slaves. Further segregation was soon achieved by removing kitchens from houses altogether and setting them among the outbuildings, which gave even modest plantations the appearance of small villages. Timber-framed and clapboard-covered tobacco barns, another New World invention, usually stood some distance from the farmhouse, adjoining the fields. Later so did "Negro quarters," hamlets of tiny cabins that mostly resembled the impermanent hovels of poor whites but sometimes were sited, often planned and always used according to African and Afro-American custom.

English vernacular buildings had become thoroughly Americanized throughout the colonies well before 1700. Traditional centers of domestic and agricultural activity remained largely unchanged — men working in farm buildings and wherever tools and crops were stored indoors, women occupying rooms where they turned raw materials into foodstuffs and textiles, and men dominating but not excluding women from domestic spaces where farm and household products were consumed. Notwithstanding, the colonial experience had the effect of consolidating those activities in New England houses efficiently organized around a central chimney while dispersing them to outbuildings and quarters on Chesapeake plantations.

It is widely believed that American architecture became more "English" again in the 18th century. This illusion arises from a failure to recognize that a new, international style of formal, genteel architecture spread all across northern Europe after 1700 and quickly reached overseas colonies as well. "Georgian" only to the Georges, this generally Palladian architecture provided standardized buildings for the many men and women who were enjoying greater social, cultural and geographical mobility than ordinary people had ever known before. They needed houses that contained not only private apartments but also public rooms laid out and furnished in ways that were recognizable to everyone who knew the rules of etiquette governing polite behavior. Local custom became less and less meaningful to the fashion conscious, and folk builders were more and more eclipsed by contractors and craftsmen whose work conformed to international canons of good taste.

Civic, religious and commercial buildings developed in the same two ways that houses had, from folk to formal and from English transplants to American hybrids. For many decades in the 17th century, colonial officials presided over public affairs from their own homes or from separate but essentially houselike structures. Similarly, merchants and storekeeping planters often set aside a room or two in their dwellings for storing and selling trade goods. Artisans' houses doubled as their workshops and showrooms. Indeed, many structures built first as houses were converted to taverns, stores, courthouses, schools and sometimes back into houses. There was a sameness to much vernacular building in early America, as there was in provincial England too.

The only specialized public buildings based on English or continental models in the 17th century were churches, nonconformist meetinghouses and an occasional covered market house in cities such as Boston. Each Protestant sect brought along a church plan and fittings suited to its own liturgy. Puritans required a prominent pulpit, movable

Corbit-Sharp House (1772 – 74), Odessa, Del., built by a wealthy Quaker tanner whose tanyard could be seen from the windows of the front parlors and a second-floor drawing room. (Winterthur Museum)

communion table and segregated seating on benches, pews or galleries arranged in a square. Quakers banished sacramental furniture and built blinds between the sexes. Anglican churchmen carried over the floor plan, altarpiece and communion rail from orthodox practice but displayed a reformed spirit in tiered pulpits for a preaching clergy and royal coats of arms to signify the union of church and state.

Church architecture conformed to standardized conventions earlier than secular buildings because religious practice had always enforced standardized observances. Architectural uniformity in other institutional and commercial structures accompanied the spread of a comprehensive code of secular rules. English-Americans learned in the 18th century to differentiate between refined public behavior and unacceptably old-fashioned folkways. Formal Palladianism provided builders with a corresponding aesthetic for many new public buildings that were needed by a growing population and run by a flourishing bureaucracy — colleges, capitols, court and custom houses, prisons and hospitals. Good taste revamped even retail stores and roadside taverns in the 18th century.

Yet, circumstances in the colonies often simplified British design. For example, county courts in North America combined the duties of several jurisdictions in

Littletown Plantation (c. 1640 –
90), James City County, Va., occupied by a Virginia official from
Essex. (Cary Carson)

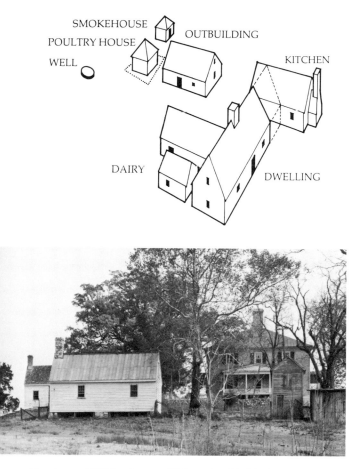

SMOKEHOUSE

POULTRY HOUSE

OUTBUILDING

WELL

KITCHEN

DAIRY

DWELLING

Slave houses (1790s) at Prestwould Plantation, Mecklenburg County, Va.,
duplexes that housed two families. A loom house and other work
buildings are closer to the main house. (HABS)

England, and many county courthouses were built with
numerous antechambers and clerks' offices to handle
paperwork and shelve records. Most colonial stores were
general stores, not specialty shops. The English distinction
among inns, taverns and alehouses was lost in the all-
purpose American "ordinary." Even New England meetinghouses, Anglicized and gentrified after the Great Awaken-
ing in the 1740s, continued to be town halls as well.

English vernacular building forms all but ceased to
influence American architecture by the end of the 17th
century. But British design shaped and reshaped commonplace buildings much longer. English influence occasionally came by way of immigrant architects — John James
to Boston, Peter Harrison to Rhode Island, James McBean (a
pupil of James Gibbs) to New York, James Porteus (William
Penn's architect) to Philadelphia, William Buckland to
Maryland, Benjamin Latrobe to Virginia and John Hawks,
the builder of Tryon Palace, to North Carolina. More often
new ideas were spread by lesser tradesmen, those who

Reconstructed Public Hospital (1770 – 73, Robert Smith), Williamsburg, Va., built by a Philadelphia master builder as the first American mental-care institution. (Colonial Williamsburg Foundation)

Middle: Third Haven Meeting-house (1684; enlarged 1797), Easton, Md. (Norman Harrington, Historical Society of Talbot County)

Above: Harvard's Massachusetts Hall (1720), Cambridge, Mass., a 32-room dormitory with individual studies. (Harvard University)

Prentis Store (1738 – 40), Williamsburg, Va., a distinctively urban building set endwise on its lot. Shelves lined the windowless side walls; a counting room was behind. (Colonial Williamsburg Foundation)

Courthouse (c. 1740), Hanover, Va., a fine brick example of a regional building type usually constructed in timber. Visitors gathered in the unusual open arcade. (Valentine Museum)

sometimes advertised themselves as "lately from Great Britain."

Pattern books were another source, used more for proportions and details than for complete designs. American builders preferred to copy one another; they borrowed from abroad only those elements that suited their own purposes. Architectural handbooks became more influential beginning in the 1790s when building tradesmen asserted the superiority of their professional architects' knowledge over clients' uneducated tastes. The authors were usually Americans, but many eagerly acknowledged their debt to leading British architects and designers from William Chambers and the brothers Adam in the 18th century to John Nash, Augustus W. N. Pugin, William Morris, Norman Shaw, Charles Voysey and Sir Edwin Lutyens into modern times. Such publications gave American buildings British pedigrees and upheld a long tradition. Almost never since the 17th century had Americans been satisfied with literal copies. Almost always British architecture was "improved" by Yankee ingenuity. ▨

FRENCH
Jay Edwards

Louisiana's Creole architecture is perhaps the most complex and elegant vernacular tradition surviving from the colonial period. The term "Creole" refers to a mixed Old World tradition, derived from European, African and perhaps Native American sources but bred locally and acclimatized to the semitropical environment of the area. No better description could be applied to Louisiana French architecture. It is a fully developed tradition, incorporating previously disparate architectural elements and ranging from tiny two-room "quarters" houses (slave dwellings) to large raised plantation houses with colonnaded galleries and sweeping hipped roofs.

The French were the major contributors to Louisiana's Creole architecture, but Native Americans, Germans, Africans, Spanish and English were not without influence. In the early 18th century, French settlers from three different backgrounds arrived simultaneously on the Mississippi Gulf Coast: settlers from France, French Canadians and French West Indian Creoles.

The Canadians provided much of the early pioneering architecture, building rectangular cabins with steeply pitched *pavilion* (hipped) roofs patterned after the houses of Quebec. They used the *poteaux en terre* method, in which posts or planks were set upright in a trench to form the walls of the house, and the *pièce sur pièce* (horizontal log) method, using full dovetail notching to fix the corners.

The settlers from France were the most architecturally sophisticated, designing simplified forms of French Renaissance houses. They adapted the traditional *colombage* (half-timber) method of framing, substituting for stones a nogging of *bousillage*, a Native American mixture of clay, lime and a binder such as Spanish moss or vegetable fiber. The early settlers of Biloxi, Mobile and New Orleans built their *bousillage entre poteaux* (mud between posts) houses

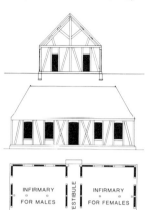

French Canadian cabin with *pavilion* roof (background), near Biloxi, Miss., shown in a 1720 sketch by Jean Baptiste le Bouteux. (Newberry Library)

Infirmary for sick blacks on a Jefferson Parish, La., plantation in 1732. *(Ministerre des Colonies)*

French colonial house (18th century), Isle of Orleans, Quebec, with the traditional *pavilion* roof that was introduced to the United States by French Canadian settlers. (Jay Edwards)

with sills laid directly on the ground in the French fashion. As a result, their dwellings rotted within only a few years.

French-speaking West Indian Creoles were much better prepared to deal with the heat and humidity of the area. By the 1720s, raised Creole houses were built in the coastal land-grant areas. One room deep, they were surrounded with open galleries and had many doors to provide a free flow of air through the interior. West Indian Creole houses were capped by a distinctive broken-pitch hipped roof — steeper in the center but less so over the surrounding galleries — and were raised on posts, often a full story above the ground, for improved ventilation. The Canadian and French settlers later modified this style. In retaining their beloved *pavilion* roof, they produced a distinctive Mississippi Valley French Creole settler's house with a steep inner roof and a sharp break in pitch about halfway between the ridge and the eaves. The sills were raised above the

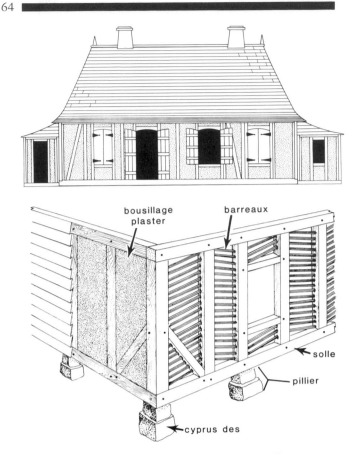

Frame wall in a *poteaux sur solle* house showing the *bousillage entre poteaux* (mud between posts) construction. (Mary Lee Eggart)

Opposite: Schreiner's boarding house (mid-18th century), St. Martinville, La., a raised Creole cottage with a broken-pitch roof. (Winterthur Museum)

ground on *piliers* (pillars) of cypress blocks, which could be knocked out and replaced when they began to rot.

About 1750 a Creole house with a single-pitch "umbrella" roof and fully built-in porch made its appearance. The earliest forms appear to have had hipped roofs; later, in the 1750s and 1760s, a gabled-roof form became popular, particularly in and around New Orleans.

Acadian (French Canadian) settlers began to arrive in New Orleans from Haiti in 1765, a decade after they had been cruelly deported en masse from Nova Scotia. They adopted as their own a gabled-roof cottage with a built-in porch — a diminutive, single-room form of the Creole house then popular in the New Orleans area and familiar to them from Haiti. Many of these houses had a stairway to the loft located on the front porch, rather than inside, as in the Louisiana Creole house. Beginning in the 1790s, a module with two rooms of equal width and two doors on the facade became the standard in many areas settled by the Acadians.

After the Revolutionary War, Anglo-Americans from the eastern seaboard and the upland South, seeking better farmland, moved to the new Louisiana territory. Other settlers from Kentucky, Ohio and Illinois lingered in St. Louis, whose Creole architecture was soon overwhelmed by Anglo-American fashion. Isolated Creole enclaves such as

Opposite: Dumont de Montigny *logement* (c. 1730), New Orleans, an early *poteaux sur solle* house with its sill directly on the ground. *(Memoires Historiques sur la Louisiane,* 1753).

Roque House (18th century), Natchitoches, La., a *bousillage entre poteaux* Creole cottage with an umbrella roof. (Courtesy J. Alfonse Prudhomme)

Creole house with a broken-pitch roof and gallery. (Mary Lee Eggart)

Ste. Genevieve, Mo., and Cahokia, Ill., survived. Simultaneously, settlers from the Carolina Tidewater established cotton plantations in the Felicianas, north of Baton Rouge, constructing raised wooden plantation houses in the fashion of the British West Indies and the Carolina Tidewater. Settlers from Virginia contributed elements of more sophisticated architectural styles that were readily adopted by the fashion-conscious Creoles.

The values of Federal and Georgian architecture were to exert a profound influence on the French Creole tradition. As early as 1790, vernacular houses with symmetrical facades were constructed by French and Spanish settlers in lower Louisiana. By the turn of the century, Creole houses exhibited fully symmetrical floor plans, and by the 1830s central halls and other features of Georgian geometry had been adopted by "proper" Creoles. Despite the popularity of these innovations, however, Creole architecture did not lose its distinctive appearance. A new variety of Creole architecture — combining Georgian geometry, Federal decorative features, and Creole roofs, walls, chimneys and galleries — established the basis for a rejuvenated Creole tradition. The Creole style still flourishes in Louisiana in the elegant re-creations of historically inspired architects, a continuation of the willingness of Creole builders to adapt their architectural heritage to an ever-changing world. ▨

Keller Plantation House (c. 1790), St. Charles Parish, La., a raised Creole plantation house with a full or single-pitch umbrella roof. (Jay Edwards)

Auguste Chouteau Mansion (1765), St. Louis, a raised Creole house built as a fur trading center. From an 1841 lithograph by J. C. Wild. (Missouri Historical Society)

Chaouachas Concession near English Turn, St. Bernard Parish, La., the earliest surviving drawing of a Louisiana indigo plantation. (Newberry Library)

Below: Raised Acadian-style house (c. 1780) on Bayou Teche, Evangeline State Park, La. (Jay Edwards)

Middle: Robert Smith House (c. 1840), Anse la Butte, La., with an outside staircase. (Jay Edwards)

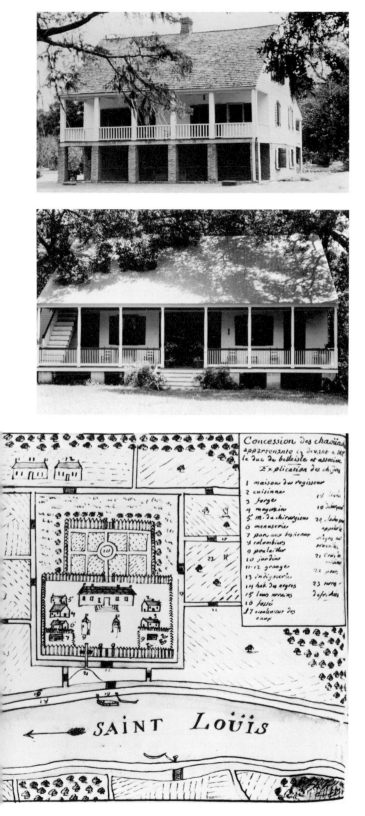

GERMANS AND SWISS
Edward A. Chappell

Most of the German-speaking people who moved to America in the late 17th and 18th centuries came from the Palatinate area of the Rhineland, the large majority first settling in southeastern Pennsylvania. Because of the considerable geographic diversity of the immigrants and prior movement of people within the Rhineland region, however, the transplanted culture was less than homogeneous. Some of the most celebrated Germanic buildings in Pennsylvania and the South, for example, were built not by immigrants from the Palatinate but by pietistic groups from Westphalia, Moravia, Bohemia and Silesia.

With few exceptions, the earliest buildings were so impermanent that now only archeological investigation can reveal anything about them. By the mid-18th century, sizable numbers of affluent German-Americans began to build houses of a quality sufficient to survive into the 20th century. These are primarily detached buildings set amid rural landholdings, more akin to the single farmsteads of minority source regions such as areas of Switzerland, Bavaria and Lower Saxony than the agricultural villages of the Palatinate. Already somewhat different in form as well as setting from their predecessors, the American houses were also recognizably distinct from those of English-speaking neighbors.

Among surviving houses in Pennsylvania and the subsequently settled areas of Maryland, Virginia and North Carolina, distinct components were often united in a form now occasionally called a *Flurküchenhaus* or, perhaps more properly, an *Ernhaus.* These buildings feature direct entry into a rectangular first-floor kitchen, with a *Stube* (square entertaining room) on the opposite side of a large internal chimney. The latter was traditionally heated by a stove vented into and provided with coals from the cooking fireplace. Particularly graphic evidence of Rhenish patterns of room use is provided by some early houses that show the scars of built-in seats around two sides of the *Stube.* Among larger houses, optional rooms included narrow sleeping chambers behind the *Stube,* additional chambers in full second stories and, less often, a small heated room at the rear of the kitchen.

Opposite: Traditional geometric painting on the interior of the R. M. Schlegel Barn (19th century), Berks County, Pa.

Centerview Farm barn, Augusta County, Va., a 19th-century forebay barn type that originated in Pennsylvania.

Roofs generally had a simple gabled form but were supported by complex framing systems paralleling those found along the Rhine. In Pennsylvania roofs were sometimes covered with flat shinglelike tiles, with the attic space used for storing grain and curing meat. This drawing together of specialized work and storage spaces in the house is more commonly illustrated by the presence of vaulted or carefully insulated cellars, sometimes incorporating a natural spring.

In the traditional Rhenish manner, builders raised walls of rubble stone or exposed heavy timber framing called *Fachwerk.* By the late 18th century, the savings in costly labor afforded by log construction made it the predominant choice despite its absence from the immediate background of most German-Americans. Log walls were a part of the vernacular building tradition in some areas of Switzerland and present-day Germany, but seldom are precise parallels for common American log joinery found there. Interiors were generally characterized by expression of building parts: Walling material was often exposed, ceiling framing was almost never hidden behind plaster, and hardware was emphasized with decorative silhouettes of a variety not seen in Anglo-American buildings of the same era.

Despite apparent similarities in the form of most early houses, others reveal no strict adherence to a single type. From New York to North Carolina, 18th-century German houses still exist that are recognizable by their parts rather than by a completely familiar form. Most significant, the kitchen sometimes lost its position as the principal entry space and was relegated to the cellar. In other cases, the kitchen remains on the first floor but the overall plan is barely distinguishable from an English or Dutch two-room house. In areas where Dutch and Germanic traits mingled early, sometimes the choice of a hillside site is the only clear evidence of German planning.

The variety of room configurations among the earliest surviving houses deserves investigation because around the end of the 18th century dramatic changes took place, reflecting powerful acculturative pressures. For perhaps a generation, essential aspects of the old forms and structures were retained but combined in ways that emphasized exterior symmetry and allowed the removal of work functions from the main floor.

Fort Zeller, Lebanon County, Pa., a mid-18th-century *Ernhaus* with a spring and food storage facilities in the cellar. This German house type was entered through the kitchen; the *Stube* was opposite a large chimney.

Front door latch at Fort Zeller, a restrained example of 18th-century German-American ironwork.

Miller's House, Millbach, Pa., probably the largest single-family German-American house surviving from the 18th century. Its form, however, is like that of smaller houses built with internal chimneys.

Snapp House (late 18th century), Shenandoah County, Va., a log three-room *Ernhaus* with direct entrance into the cooking room on the left.

Yancy House (late 18th century), Rockingham County, Va., a three-room *Ernhaus* with a central chimney serving as a cooking fireplace for the kitchen at right.

Spangler House, Lebanon County, Pa., an 18th-century stone house of incontestable German credentials and appearance but not an *Ernhaus* form.

Kitchen of the Philip Dellinger House (c. 1815), Shenandoah County, Va. The exposed ceiling framing, masonry fireplace and log walls are typical of German immigrants' tendency to express individual building parts.

Detail of an iron door strap on a
smokehouse at Tulpehocken
Manor, Lebanon County, Pa., an
example of the German affinity for
rich decoration of mundane
objects.

Stove in the Schiefferstadt House
(mid-18th century), Frederick, Md.
This five-plate cast-iron stove was
a type commonly used to heat the
Stube and remains in its original
location on the house's upper
floor.

Michael Braun House, Rowan County, N.C., an example showing changes
in building design resulting from late 18th-century acculturation.

Henry Glassie has suggested that the Pennsylvania
farmhouses with two facade doors built well into the 19th
century were still influenced by memories of the German
plan. In Virginia's Shenandoah Valley, lingering evidences of
Rhenish planning were almost entirely abandoned, and for
those wealthy enough to build on a substantial scale, the
all-American center-passage I house became the predictable
choice. Among the affluent, distance from their past was
further established by using brick or weatherboarded frame
walls, leaving log and stone for work buildings and for the
one- and two-room houses of their less successful neighbors. The change in materials is highly evident in Salem,
N.C., settled by Moravians in 1766. In 1769, for example, a
large dormitory for single men was built with *Fachwerk*
walls; in 1786 both a dormitory for single women and an
addition to the men's building were constructed with
Flemish-bond brick walls.

During the earliest decades of the 19th century, when a
homogeneous American form overwhelmed recognizable
German forms, the decoration of interiors and furnishings

R. S. Lam House, Augusta County, Va., a quintessential American I house type that replaced the *Ernhaus* for most affluent German families in 19th-century Virginia. (All previous photos by Edward A. Chappell)

Single Brothers' House (1769), Salem, N.C., a Moravian *Fachwerk* building extended by a brick addition in 1786. (Old Salem, Inc.)

was carried to a level of richness and flamboyance previously unknown. To some degree this phenomenon was a reflection of a widespread stylistic trend toward the imaginative use of decorative, nonfunctional woodwork, achieved principally through the manipulation of Adamesque design formulas. More important, the new woodwork and decorative painting expressed the presence of an aesthetic not shared by most other Americans.

This seeming dichotomy between exterior conformity and interior expressiveness raises more general questions of how minority groups respond to pressures exerted by those who maintain political and economic dominance. In the strongest areas of 18th-century German ancestry, there are still remarkable traces of minority culture ranging from the occasional use of dialect to the painting of barns with large-scale traditional motifs. These are now mere vestiges. When earlier German-Americans faced great pressure to conform, they responded with an intense although largely personal expression of affection for old cultural distinctions. ▦

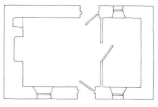

Above and right: Northwest Irish house (mid-19th century), County Galway, Ireland, the basic form of the ancient Celtic house — two rooms with an end fireplace and opposed doors. (All photographs and plans, Henry Glassie)

Stone Irish-American house (early 19th century), Loudoun County, Va., reflecting Irish form.

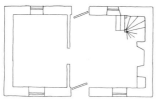

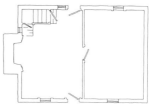

Plan of a stone Irish-American house (c. 1820), Frederick County, Md., repeating the northwest Irish plan. The loft with a stair is a common American modification of the one-story Irish plan.

Plan of a log Irish-American house (c.1830), Greene County, Pa., with a protruding chimney.

Opposite: Log Irish-American house (mid-19th century), Greene County, Tenn.

IRISH
Henry Glassie

In a small white house on a green hill in Ireland, the old
farmer sits with his cracked hands on his knees. His eyes
are closed. His song lifts through the dark at his hearth:

Farewell my old acquaintance, my friends both one and
all.
My lot is in America, to either rise or fall.
From my cabin I'm evicted and likewise compelled to go
From that lovely land called Erin, where the green
shamrocks grow.

Steady, he glides into the chorus, erasing joy from the text
with a melancholy minor air: .

Hurray, my boys, the sails is spread and the wind is
blowing fair.
Full steam for Castle Garden, in a few days we'll be
there.
For to seek for bread and labor, as we are compelled to go
From that lovely land called Erin, where the green
shamrocks grow.

Laments for the exiles from Erin recount the causes that
sent millions out of Ireland across a dreadful ocean: the
rackrenting landlord, eviction, famine, political struggle,
the wish for religious freedom, the need for land and labor.
In two great waves the Irish came, each time forming the
vanguard in a new American experience.

The Irish immigrants of the early 18th century are
usually called Scotch-Irish. Many were descendants of the
Scots planted in Ulster in the 17th century, although they
were a diverse population of farming people, largely Protestant, who left northern Ireland to claim the vast Appa-
lachian frontier as their domain. The second wave of Irish
immigration carried people, primarily Catholics from the
south, into the great American cities. There they created
the distinct atmosphere of the ethnic neighborhood.

The architectural record of Irish immigration is not a
matter of monuments that stand in isolation on a homogeneous American landscape. Rather, in the 18th century the
Irish, English and Germans combined to build America.
The Irish contribution is difficult to distinguish because it
was integral to the formation of the American whole. The
farm on the frontier in its solitary setting with its log house
and scattering of outbuildings, whether erected by the Irish
or not, meshed Irish, English and German traditions into
something new. Generally, the barn and dominant techniques of wood construction rose out of the German

Irish-American linear farm (19th century), Cumberland County, Pa., retaining Old World unity in the precise alignment of the house and barn.

Linear farm (early 19th century), County Fermanagh, Northern Ireland. In early days the house and cow barn were part of a single, long building, which later broke apart to create a neat linear arrangement of separate shelters for people and animals.

tradition, while the stone masonry and form of the house were sometimes English, sometimes Irish. Even that conclusion is too simple. The characteristic house of northern and western Ireland — its interior partitioned into a large heated room entered immediately from the exterior and a smaller unheated room (for chilled sleeping) — became the characteristic house of the frontier, but its form was known as well in Scotland, Wales and western England. The Irish tradition was shared with Britain as part of an ancient Celtic heritage. And the Celtic cultures were part of a widespread European mountain tradition, so the linear layout of farms in Ulster was paralleled not only in Wales but also in Germanic Europe. Farms trimly arranged in a line on the valley slopes that run southwestward out of Pennsylvania signal an American pattern with antecedents in Switzerland and Ulster, attributable less to the retention of Old World ideas than to the flexible, synthetic spirit of the frontier.

The Irish dimension in the architecture of the American frontier is not a matter of a few discrete forms but of an approach to space generated from social values. The Appalachian log house and later the sod house of the Great Plains repeated the old Celtic form: a welcoming open door that brought the visitor immediately to the hospitable hearth. Outside, the working buildings were arranged close by, frankly stating the farm's functions. Beyond the cleared fields, the wilderness rolled and howled. The separately

Middle: Independent farm,
County Down, Northern Ireland.
Such isolated farms have been a
feature of the Irish landscape since
prehistoric times.

Above: Independent farm (late
19th century), Upshur County,
W.Va., an isolated farm with the
white house and the unpainted
outbuildings fanning uphill.

Below: Terraced row, Enniskillen, County Fermanagh, Northern Ireland. The English townhouse, terraced in rows, is typical of Irish cities and towns.

Opposite: Whitewashed interior of a log house (early 19th century), Shenandoah County, Va., recalling the interiors of Irish houses.

Terraced row, "The Pocket," Philadelphia, an old Irish neighborhood containing impeccably kept houses in neat rows.

Detail of stone chimney of a log house, Greene County, Pa., representing continuity of an Irish skill.

sited American farm, essential to our national tradition of privacy that survives in suburban planning, has one of its sources in the enclosures that massively reorganized the English landscape, replacing compact, cooperative villages with dispersed, independent and profitable farmsteads. But the Irish had always lived on separate farms. Their famil-iarity with the idea of a lone farm asserted into the wilderness on which the nuclear family formed the basic social unit made them the natural leaders of the Appa-lachian invasion, and the independent family farm, so fundamental to American social history, can be read as a direct translation to the New World of an elder Irish tradition.

The potato crop failure of 1846–47 swept away a quarter of Ireland's population. They died on the roadside. They filled the ships to America and pioneered the urban frontier, filling the row houses of eastern cities and shaping political structures in the factories, taprooms and ethnic clubhouses that would be adopted by later immigrants from southern and eastern Europe. Their houses were built on a model developed in London, then transferred to Dublin, Belfast and a host of provincial Irish towns. The plan was like that of the Celtic country house — two rooms, the larger entered immediately — but turned with the end to the street and shifted beneath the gable to form a terraced row. This is the home of urban workers throughout the English-speaking world — of Pakistanis in London, of Italians in Philadelphia.

But the old Irish neighborhoods remain distinct. While members of other groups push individuality into the facade, the Irish join their neighbors in uncluttered clarity, unifying the faces of their homes in pure white detail. The white cornices of the Irish block recall the whitewash that hid the brown logs of their frontier homes and the whitewash layered over the stone of their old homes in green Erin.

Twice pioneers, first in the mountainy woodlands in the 18th century and second in the smoky cities of the 19th, the Irish took hold of the American tradition and made it their own. They did not create oddities out of which scholars can create symbols of their architectural contribu-tion. Instead, they built their heritage into the American style. 🔲

RUSSIANS
Anatole Senkevitch, Jr.

Sparked by Vitus Bering's exploratory voyage in 1741, Russian settlement of the northwestern portion of the North American continent was a result of Russia's eastward expansion, motivated primarily by a quest for a more lucrative maritime fur trade. The first *promyshlenniki* (Russian fur hunters and traders) to reach the Aleutian Islands put up temporary structures of driftwood, the only source of timber. These structures ranged from flimsy makeshift dwellings to the more substantial adaptations of native Aleut *yurts* that made up the first permanent Russian settlement of Illiuliuk, or Good Harmony (now Unalaska), founded in the mid-1700s on Unalaska Island.

More consequential in shaping the Russian colonial building tradition was the architecture that began emerging a decade later in the Kodiak Island and parts beyond. Built almost entirely of wood, these later settlements perpetuated the traditional Russian method of log construction — a frame of logs laid horizontally on a rectangular or polygonal plan and secured at the corners through interlocking ends. This rapid, virtually prefabricated method of construction allowed the development of expressive building forms within the context of an underlying traditionalism.

The more immediate source for the architecture of Russian America, however, was the utilitarian building tradition established in the harsh environment of eastern Siberia, the staging area for the countless fur hunting and trading expeditions to northwestern America. Accordingly, most settlements in Russian America evoked the more austere architectural style of the eastern Siberian *ostrog*

Sitka, Alaska, in 1827. The ubiquitous *izby* (log cabins with steep hipped roofs) surrounded the first Church of St. Michael (1817), a tiered, octagonal style popular in Russia. *(Partie Historique Atlas,* 1835)

(stockaded town), whose log buildings reflected an expedient manipulation of form and detail.

The establishment of full-fledged Russian colonial settlements, usually sited atop promontories, at the mouths of rivers or at the heads of bays along the mainland and insular coasts, was spearheaded by an Irkutsk merchant. In 1784 Grigori I. Shelikhov established Three Saints Harbor on the southwestern coast of Kodiak Island as his company's first and primary settlement. However, the shortage of timber there led to the founding of St. Paul Harbor on the island's northeast coast in 1791 and the transfer of company headquarters there the following year. Built on a steep, rocky beach, St. Paul Harbor (now Kodiak) at first consisted of an extended semicircular wooden fort containing barracks, administrative offices and a fur storage warehouse. By 1840 a complex of shops, warehouses and smithies as well as an infirmary, a church and a series of houses had been added, giving more definitive shape to what became the first capital and one of the largest settlements of Russian America.

Other settlements followed. The most noteworthy architecturally were the two forts on neighboring Afognak Island and the Kenai (Cook) Inlet that Shelikhov founded in 1796. Their designs, combining traditional Siberian woodbuilding techniques and the striking geometric regularity so favored by the late 18th-century Russian neoclassical architects, projected a degree of durability and decorum far more elaborate than that of any other Russian-American outpost.

Russian adaptation of an Aleut dwelling (c. 1828), Good Harmony. The settlers raised the oval huts to ground level, moved the entrance from the roof top and added window glazing. *(Partie Historique Atlas)*

Petropavlovsk, Alaska, in 1803, with austere log cabins based on Siberian prototypes. (Kruzenshtern's *Atlas*, 1813)

Rhomboid and triangular forts founded by Shelikhov at Afognak Island (top) and Kenai Inlet (bottom). (A. I. Andreev, 1948)

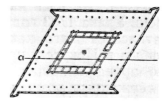

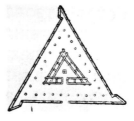

Left: Chapel at Fort Ross, Calif., since reconstructed after a 1970 fire. (HABS)

The next phase of Russian colonial settlement began in 1799 with the formation of the Russian-American Company, which monopolized Russian settlement and trade in America. Heading south in search of a more abundant supply of sea otter pelts, Alexander Baranov, the Russian colony's first governor, founded New Archangel on Baranof Island off the Alaska panhandle. Established to offset American and English trade with the Tlingits and take advantage of the site's abundant timber supply and suitable tides, New Archangel (later Sitka) quickly became the center of the company's fur trade; in 1808 it became the colonial capital. Built on a steep, rocky promontory projecting into the inlet, the fort constituting the nucleus of New Archangel consisted of the governor's house, a large barracks and warehouses set within a wooden stockade reinforced by hewn-log towers. A linear main street lined with the ubiquitous Russian log cabins linked the town beyond to a parade ground situated at the edge of the fort.

The second step in the Russian-American Company's march southward was the founding of an outpost on the California coast, which the Russians occupied for only 29 years. Fort Ross was established in 1821 just north of San Francisco Bay as a base for hunting sea otter and growing food. Its first hewn-log buildings, which included the commandant's house, a fur warehouse, a kitchen and barracks, were constructed within the protective walls of a stockade, with only two blockhouses built at the northeast and southwest corners. A simple but expressive chapel was erected in the 1820s, with two of its sides incorporating the stockade wall.

With the relative consolidation of the Russian colony in the mid-19th century came efforts, chiefly in New Archangel, to produce a more stylish colonial architecture. The numerous buildings erected in this period were charming variations of the provincial Russian classical revival in wood, incorporating lunettes, pilasters and classical fenestration. Using traditional hewn-log construction, these buildings were often sheathed in clapboarding, thus making them appear more formal. The most striking neoclassical monument of Russian colonial architecture is St. Michael's Cathedral (1844) in New Archangel, a blend of simplified neoclassical elements and native Russian architectural motifs.

Yet, despite such isolated efforts to impart style to Russian colonial architecture, virtually all of the settlements in Russia's American colony proved to be little more than frontier "company" towns. The Russian-American Company's almost obsessive preoccupation with fur trading supplied little incentive for constructing, for the most part, anything more than expedient structures. The decline of the maritime fur trade by the 1850s severely undermined the status of the Russian colony as a commercial enterprise, a fact that prompted its eventual sale to the United States in 1867. Although most Russian colonial buildings have long since disappeared, vestiges are still discernible in a few surviving structures in parts of Alaska, the Aleutian Islands and California. These structures include a number of Russian Orthodox churches and some early buildings obscured by subsequent additions and modifications; a few have been restored or reconstructed. ▨

Opposite: Fort Ross, Calif., in 1828. Located outside the fort were a bathhouse and stables as well as workshops and houses of Aleut trappers, who preferred the Russian-style cabins. (*Voyage autour du Monde,* 1835)

Sitka, seen in 1867, shortly after Alaska was sold to the United States.
Dominating the skyline of the compact frontier capital are the governor's
mansion and St. Michael's Cathedral. (Peter S. Duval and Son, 1869)

Sitka Bay and the Russian-American Company fur warehouses in 1827.
The temple-front motif was then as prevalent in Russia as the Greek
Revival was in America. *(Partie Historique Atlas)*

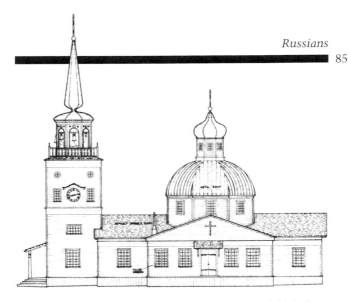

St. Michael's Cathedral (1844), Sitka. This neoclassical landmark has a traditional Russian onion dome. (Robert G. Higginbotham, HABS)

Lincoln Street, Sitka, about 1901, looking toward the cathedral. At right is the Old Trading Post (c. 1808), a log building with a massive hipped roof built by the Russian-American Company. It became the Sitka Trading Company after 1867 but was torn down about 1920. (Library of Congress)

Parade grounds in Sitka about 1890. Flanking the governor's mansion were company offices (remodeled) and a barracks, both used by the U.S. government. All are now gone. (Sitka Historical Society Museum)

SOUTHEASTERN SPANISH
Kathleen Deagan

The Spanish were the first Europeans to build in what is now the United States. For 250 years Spanish colonists, soldiers and priests settled along the southern boundary, from Florida to California. They developed a distinctive Spanish-American cultural tradition, shaped by their efforts to retain a familiar way of life in the face of isolation and an unfamiliar environment.

The first Spanish settlement in the United States was St. Augustine, Fla., the oldest European city in the country. It was established in 1565 as a military outpost and mission center and served as the capital of Spanish Florida for 250 years. During that time, the Spanish presence extended at different times as far north as Virginia and westward along the Gulf Coast into Louisiana. The town of Santa Elena (now Parris Island), S.C., was the capital of Spanish Florida from 1566 to 1576, and Spanish cultural influence is still evident in the region in other cities such as Pensacola, Fla., which was under Spanish rule from 1698 to 1763 and from 1781 to 1821. As in the Southwest, Spanish settlements in Florida were primarily military and religious outposts. Spain's rule ended in 1821, but its architectural legacy remains visible today.

The use of space by Spanish colonists throughout the New World was predictably organized and relatively unchanging through time. Formal ordinances for city planning were established by 1573, based on a Rennaissance-influenced grid plan. Streets were arranged at right angles to one another, forming blocks around or adjacent to a plaza on which important public buildings stood. Examples of this grid plan can be seen today in the colonial sections of St. Augustine, Pensacola and San Juan, Puerto Rico. The blocks created by the streets were divided into regularly sized lots, within which the Spanish colonists organized space and lot elements in a consistent arrangement. Houses fronted directly on the streets and were usually set in an enclosed compound with entry through a gate in the lot wall rather than directly into the house. The kitchen, wells and areas for gardening, livestock and trash disposal were located within the lot enclosure. Archeological evidence

Detail from a 1586 engraving of St. Augustine, Fla., showing its traditional Spanish grid plan with important buildings on the plaza. A similar plan was used in Santa Fe. (St. Augustine Historical Society)

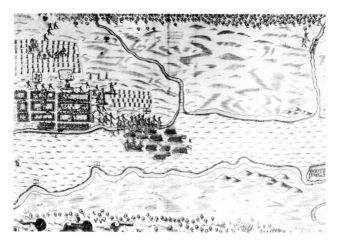

from sites in Florida and the Caribbean reveals that this Spanish spatial pattern was adhered to faithfully from the 16th to the 19th centuries.

Vernacular domestic architecture in the Spanish colonial borderlands followed a general pattern, with certain distinct local modifications. This pattern was based on a humble prototype found widely in rural Spain and in European peasant communities. It consists of a basic rectangular structure of one or two multipurpose, interconnecting rooms, usually with a *loggia* (covered porch) on the south or east side to take advantage of the sun and prevailing breezes. The earliest such buildings documented in Florida and the Caribbean were constructed of wattle and daub (clay daubed over a basketlike wood and twig framework) or boards with thatched roofs; later examples were of tabby, a cementlike mixture of oyster shells, lime, water and sand, or coquina stone, a local sedimentary rock formed by compacting periwinkle shells. When made of stone or adobe, these houses typically had flat roofs; when constructed of wood or wattle and daub, they had pitched thatched roofs.

More elaborate houses built on the basic rectangular unit plan by adding rooms, most often in single-file rows. These could be arranged to form wings opening onto a patio, often with adjacent porches faced by a portico of arches. Detached kitchens were also characteristic of these expanded versions of the common-plan house. Eighteenth-century examples in Florida usually had balconies on the street side, constructed on second-floor joists that protruded through the wall to the house exterior. A similar construction form is found in the Canary Islands, from which settlers emigrated to Florida in the early 18th century.

Plan of Pensacola, Fla., in 1813, when most of the land within the fort was subdivided to raise money for the local civil government. The area is now known as Seville Square. (Special Collections, University of West Florida)

Early sketch of Pensacola, which was ruled by Spain from 1698 to 1763 and 1781 to 1821. (Special Collections, University of West Florida)

Llambia House, St. Augustine. This example of a late 18th-century colonial home of a prosperous family is built of plastered local shellstone (coquina). The patio entrance is on the side. (James Quine, St. Augustine Historical Society)

Windows in Spanish colonial Florida often had sills supported by a step projecting into the street and covered by a *reja* (wooden grating). This provided a protected bay window from which, according to tradition, Spanish ladies could discreetly observe the outside world.

Interior spaces in frontier Spanish houses were typically spare and simple, with whitewashed walls; humble houses had earthen floors, while more substantial houses used tile or wood. Houses in colonial Florida generally did not have hearths or chimneys but rather were heated with a charcoal brazier. Furnishings typically consisted of a few pieces of heavy carved wood furniture, such as chests, benches and a table. The *horno* (a waist-high, platformlike Spanish masonry stove) was used in Florida houses, in contrast to the *fogon* (a very low hearth in the corner fireplace) and a beehive-shaped exterior oven that were found in southwestern structures.

Because of the frontier nature of Spanish settlements in the United States, few trained architects were present, and little of the architecture can be considered high style. Even the most notable nondomestic architecture — the town and

Opposite: De Hita Houses, St. Augustine. Reconstructed on the basis of archeological evidence, they are typical houses of about 1700. The structure at left is plastered tabby, that at right plastered coquina block. The window is covered by a *reja*. (James Quine)

Conjectural drawings of a 16th-century wattle-and-daub common house in St. Augustine, based on research and plans by Albert Manucy. (James Quine)

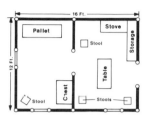

Peck House, St. Augustine. Restored to its appearance about 1750, a portico of arches along the *loggia* faces a patio. (James Quine, Historic St. Augustine Preservation Board)

Oldest House, St. Augustine. Reconstructed to the 1700 period, the house's interior is typically simple, with whitewashed walls and little furniture. A charcoal brazier is for heating. (James Quine, St. Augustine Historical Society)

mission churches — were designed and built by priests rather than by architects. Although they generally conform in floor plan to traditional Catholic church precepts, they consistently incorporated modifications required by the use of local materials and Native American laborers.

Military architecture was probably the most formal expression of Spanish colonial building in the Southeast and the Caribbean. The earliest forts in Florida were triangular constructions of earth and wood, surrounded by moats. These were replaced during the 17th and 18th centuries by stone fortifications such as the still intact Castillo de San Marcos (1672–96) and Fort Matanzas (1740) in St. Augustine and Fort San Carlos de Barrancas (1787) in Pensacola. These later forts were constructed by military engineers and were influenced to a great extent by prevailing design in European military architecture, notably that associated with the Italian Bautista Antonelli. The great fortresses of San Juan, including El Morro (1539) and its associated fortifications, reflect more than 200 years of construction, renovation and expansion.

Another Spanish-influenced architectural style that occurs widely in Florida and the Southwest is the Mediterranean (Spanish colonial) Revival style, popular in the 1920s. These buildings, characterized by clay tile roofs, textured stucco exteriors, arch motifs and ornamental ironwork, were the inspiration of 20th-century American architects rather than a direct heritage of the Spanish colonists.

The Spanish colonial experience in North America was for the most part one of frontier adaptation. Living precariously between the rich Spanish empire to the south and a vast, often hostile continent to the north, Spanish colonists developed a style of life and architecture based on traditional Spanish forms with adjustments made to local materials, climate and building traditions. Although the Spaniards left the United States in 1821, the influences of their architectural and cultural traditions still exist along its southern borders and provide a key element in the distinctive regional flavor of the Gulf and southwestern states. ◼

Cathedral of St. Augustine (1797), a modified Latin cross shape. The original church, whose entrance was flanked by paired Doric columns and a two-tier *espanada,* was gutted by fire in 1887 and later restored by James Renwick. (St. Augustine Historical Society)

Castillo de San Marcos (1672 – 96), St. Augustine, one of the later Spanish forts influenced by European designs. (James Quine)

El Cañuelo (c. 1520), Cabras Island, San Juan, Puerto Rico, an early Spanish fort of fieldstone covered with plaster. (Frederick C. Gjessing, HABS)

Mar-a-Lago (1927, Marion Sims Wyeth), Palm Beach, Fla., one of the most lavishly decorated examples of the Mediterranean Revival style in the region. (Jack E. Boucher, HABS)

SOUTHWESTERN HISPANICS
Joe S. Graham

The Southwest's distinctive architectural heritage was forged primarily during the Spanish colonial period (1540–1821) and the Mexican period (1821–48). Spanish settlement of the Southwest began with Coronado's exploration of the region in 1540–42. With their missions, *presidios* (forts) and secular settlements, missionaries and soldiers began the tremendous task of converting and Hispanisizing the native populations of the region. By 1680 the 2,500 Spanish colonists then living in New Mexico were driven out during the Pueblo Revolt. During the 1690s New Mexico was retaken by the Spanish, exploration of Texas, California and Arizona began again, and missions and *presidios* were established, a process that continued for more than a century and a half. By Mexican independence in 1821, there were between 25,000 and 30,000 Spanish in the Southwest. When it became U.S. territory in 1848, an estimated 80,000 Mexicans in the region became U.S. citizens. Mexican immigration has dramatically swelled the Hispanic population in the region to seven or eight million today.

Many towns and cities in the Southwest can trace their history to one of three principal settlement types of the Spanish colonial era: *villas*, *ranchos* and *plazas*. According to the Spanish Law of the Indies (1573), *villas*, formally organized towns such as Santa Fe and Los Angeles, were laid out in grids with parallel streets, usually around a central plaza, fortified by walls for defense. The central plaza often had the church at one end and government buildings at the other.

Some towns evolved from *haciendas*, which were more common in California than in New Mexico or Texas. The *haciendas* often consisted of the main house of the *patron* (landowner) surrounded by the houses of the *peones* (laborers) and *vaqueros* (cowboys) and often a church and a school.

Because of Native American hostilities, many rural dwellers consolidated for mutual defense into *plazas*, small fortified villages made up of houses placed contiguously around and facing a plaza with one *zaguan* (entry gate) and *torreones* (towers for defense) at the corners. The outside walls had no windows or doors, so that the settlers, when under attack, could put their livestock into the *plaza* and close the entry gate, creating an easily defensible community. In the early 19th century, there were more than a hundred *plazas* in New Mexico, including Taos.

The Spanish introduced a number of important technologies into southwestern architecture. Building techniques included making adobe brick (which rapidly replaced the Native Americans' hand-shaped turtleback adobes and puddling construction), improving techniques for building the flat roofs so characteristic of adobe architecture in the Southwest, making and using lime in construction, using curved red clay tiles for roofing, cutting and building with stone and using corner-notched log construction and the palisade wall structure typical of much east Texas ecclesiastical architecture and fortifications. Other significant contributions included the Roman arch, corbels, wood and stone carving for decoration, dome and vaulted ceilings and roofs, hooded and bell-shaped fireplaces, and the *zambullo* door, made of hand-split lumber and a pintle hinge,

Top and above: San Xavier del Bac (1791), near Tuscon, Ariz. One of the
more elaborate missions in the Southwest, this was built under the
direction of two architects, the Gaona brothers. Its cruciform plan
features a complex system of domes and vaults, curved parapets, towers
and an elaborate entrance contrasting with plain walls, all covered with
bright white lime plaster. In the highly decorated chapel can be seen
retablos and *bultos*. (Both, HABS)

Above and right: Church of St. Francis of Assisi, Ranchos de Taos, N.M. A cruciform structure with heavy buttressed walls built in the early 18th century and rebuilt about 1780, this church represented a change from earlier single-aisle designs and is considered one of the finest examples of the Spanish-Pueblo style. (T. Harmon Parkhurst, Museum of New Mexico; Walter Smalling, HABS)

Penitente *morada*, Abiquiu, N.M., a small church built by the community using adobe and *vigas*. (Bill Lippincott, Museum of New Mexico)

Mission Nuestra Señora de la Purisima Concepcion de Acuña (1731), San Antonio, Tex. Made of stone with lime and sand mortar, this mission with two bell towers is typical of Texas and California designs. (William Peoples, HABS)

Mission Santa Barbara (1792, 1814–20), Santa Barbara, Calif. Typical of the California missions are the *campanario* for the bells and low-pitched gabled roofs of curved red tile.

consisting of pins at bottom and top used as pivots. The bright colors — especially aqua — that characterize houses in Mexican-American communities today can be traced to earlier Hispanic architecture.

The most spectacular architectural monuments in the Southwest are the missions, most built by the Franciscans with the help of mission Indians. The earliest were built in New Mexico in the 1620s, and the last was completed in 1823 in California. Constructed with the materials at hand, the missions in each subregion had a distinctive style. New Mexico missions were a combination of Spanish and Pueblo style and technique. Their massive walls of adobe, plastered inside and out for many centuries, acquired a gentle upward slope with soft rounded corners. The flat roofs were supported by heavy *vigas* (exposed beams), covered with pieces of wood arranged in a herringbone pattern and finished with a thick layer of mud. These churches had a center aisle, and the facade was often flanked by double towers or capped with a belfry.

Missions in Texas, Arizona and California were made mostly of stone laid in a mortar of lime and sand. Texas and Arizona missions had domed or vaulted roofs; windows and doors, as well as facades, were often ornately decorated. The Texas missions incorporated more obvious elements of high-style Mexican church architecture, such as elaborate

Plan for a typical New Mexican *hacienda.* Sometimes called the *casa-corral,* this structure was built for defense; the outside walls had no doors or windows, and defenders could shoot from atop the flat roofs. Many similar buildings did not have the separate livestock area. (Based on plan by Bainbridge Bunting)

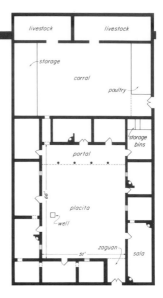

Reconstruction of an 18th-century New Mexican room at the Smithsonian Institution. The handmade furnishings were simple and sparse. The ceiling *cajas* have a herringbone pattern. (Smithsonian Institution)

baroque *churrigueresque* carvings in the style of José Benito de Churriguera (1665–1725), a Spanish architect whose style of baroque opulence greatly influenced Mexican church architecture.

The California missions were established in the late 18th and early 19th centuries and were often quite elaborate, such as those at San Juan Capistrano and San Luis Rey. Moorish elements can be seen in the arches and arched windows of many churches. Adobe construction and the use of painting rather than tile or stone for interior decoration are local adaptations. A characteristic feature of many of these missions as well as of those in Texas is a *campanario* (a vertical wall projection with cutouts to hold the mission's bells). California missions had low-pitched roofs of red burned clay tile on wooden frameworks, typical in Spain and parts of Mexico. While many roofs had wide projecting eaves, others had curved, pedimented gables.

As a rule, the massive walls of the churches, whether of plastered adobe or bare stone, were decorated toward the front with paintings, altar screens, *retablos* (folk paintings of the saints) and *bultos* (carved figures of the saints). Some were quite splendid. The small churches and chapels found in small southwestern towns were built with community labor and without architects. The Penitente *moradas* (houses of worship) are unique to New Mexico and the San Luis Valley of Colorado, although small *oratorios* (small chapels used for prayer) are common among the rural Hispanic Catholics in the region.

Some of the oldest public architecture in the United

Bell-shaped fireplace in a Penitente *morada* chapel kitchen (1852), Arroyo Hondo, N.M. Although usually smaller than this one, similar fireplaces introduced by the Spanish were standard in New Mexican homes. (Jack E. Boucher, HABS)

Plaza del Cerro, Chimayo, N.M. In the *plaza* town configuration, all buildings were contiguous, forming a closed square with one wide gate *(zaguan)* leading outside. Doors and windows were on the plaza side for protection. At right is a private chapel (Melinda Bell, Museum of New Mexico)

House in Chamisal, N.M., receiving a new application of adobe in 1940. (Russell Lee, Library of Congress)

South Texas *jacal*, about 1900. A first-generation folk house used in the region until the 1930s, *jacales* had steeply pitched gabled roofs, supported by a ridge pole in the center and *vigas* on the sides. This style was imported from the interior of Mexico and diffused by Spanish colonists. (Joe S. Graham Collection)

Cooper-Molera Adobe (c. 1823), Monterey, Calif., a Monterey-style walled house with a low hipped roof shading a second-story balcony. (Joshua Freiwald)

Right: Museum of Fine Arts (1917, Rapp and Rapp), Santa Fe, a good example of contemporary Spanish-Pueblo style. (State of New Mexico)

Laboratory of Anthropology (1931, John Gaw Meem), Santa Fe. This 20th-century building recalls the Southwest's architectural heritage in its massive adobe walls, *vigas. portal* and other details. (Ansel Adams, Museum of New Mexico)

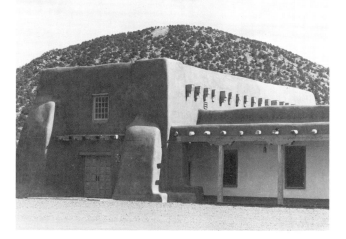

States, too, is Spanish. The Palace of the Governors (1610), in Santa Fe, although it has been damaged and rebuilt many times since 1680, is still in use today. The Governor's Palace (1749) in San Antonio is another excellent example of this type of public architecture. As important as the mission in the cultural conquest of the Southwest, the Spanish *presidio*, borrowed from the Moors, was so successful that Americans later copied it in places such as Bent's Fort in Colorado.

The first-generation folk houses were *jacales*, used in the region into the 1930s. Borrowed from indigenous groups in Mexico and spread throughout Spanish Texas by early Spanish colonists, the south Texas *jacales* had steeply pitched thatched roofs. The flat-roofed New Mexico style, found as far south as the Big Bend of Texas, evolved from Native American structures. Second-generation folk architecture consisted principally of small flat-roofed adobe buildings of one, two or three rooms, almost invariably with hard-packed dirt floors. In recent years, many flat roofs have been covered with gabled roofs or wood shingles or galvanized steel. In south Texas, second-generation folk housing consisted of the small board-and-batten structures built on the model of the earlier *jacales* but using technology and material from the Anglo South. These houses were often enlarged, growing as family size dictated and economics permitted. Cooking was done outside, for the most part with baking carried out in dome-shaped ovens.

Wealthier people lived in more spacious houses, often L-shaped and usually one room deep and several rooms long. Large *haciendas*, although relatively rare, were often modeled on Mexican *haciendas*. Some New Mexican types were designed with the typical *placita* (small enclosed area), with one entry gate. South Texas *haciendas* were fortified houses with thick walls of *ciar* (blocks of hard caliche clay cut from veins close to the surface). The buildings of San Ygnacio, near Laredo, Tex., are excellent examples of this style.

Spanish colonial architecture has left a profound imprint on the cultural landscape of the Southwest. It has been the basis for the major regional architectural styles, including the Monterey style of California and the Spanish colonial style found in California and Texas. One of the most distinctive is the Santa Fe (also called Spanish-Pueblo) style of New Mexico, evident, for example, in the Museum of Fine Arts (1917, Rapp and Rapp), Museum of New Mexico, and the Laboratory of Anthropology (1931, John Gaw Meem).

Adobe brick remains a popular building material, and the flat roofs or low-pitched red tile roofs may be found in both elite and popular architecture. The Roman arches appear in every type of building imaginable, from houses to Mexican food establishments and even filling stations, as well as many public buildings. The rambling house one room deep built around a partially enclosed patio fathered the popular and ubiquitous "ranch" style so popular in the Southwest. The small flat-roofed adobe structures of the Southwest have become synonymous with the term "Spanish Southwest" and are perhaps the dominant single architectural presence in the region. ▨

Opposite: Palace of the Governors (1610), Santa Fe, the oldest U.S. public building. Its flat-roofed adobe form with a front *portal* helped create a lasting regional architecture. (State of New Mexico)

BELGIANS
Charles F. Calkins and William G. Laatsch

Between 1853 and 1857, Walloon-speaking Belgian immigrants from the provinces of Brabant, Hainaut and Namur settled in northeastern Wisconsin on the Door Peninsula. By 1860, 3,812 foreign-born Belgians lived in the area, forming the largest rural Walloon settlement area in the United States. This settlement was one of many formed by either Walloons or Flemings who found their way to the states around Lake Michigan — particularly Wisconsin, Michigan and Illinois — beginning about 1850 and continuing to the end of the century. As these pioneers gained a hold on the land in Wisconsin, a distinctive ethnic cultural landscape emerged. The hallmarks of the architectural forms introduced by the Belgians include the brick house, outdoor bake oven, roadside chapel and Belgian barn.

The modest red brick farmhouses of the Belgians contrast with the frame and clapboard structures that characterize most of northeastern Wisconsin. In many cases the brick is only a veneer masking massive logs that provide the real structure of the house. Most of the farmhouses were built of logs and date from 1872, when northeastern Wisconsin experienced a building boom following a severe forest fire. Later, as recently as 1949, the logs were covered by brick, perhaps as a fire retardant or for weather proofing. Red brick was not used exclusively, however. Cream City brick, shipped from Milwaukee, was often chosen as decoration for windows, doors, gables and quoins.

Given the size limitation imposed by the log lengths, these houses are unpretentious. The ground floor typically accommodates a large kitchen, pantry, parlor and a small sleeping room or two. The second floor is devoted entirely to sleeping areas and is dominated by a dormitory-style room and two or three partitioned bedrooms. A notable detail is the circular or semicircular window situated high on the gable facing the road. Functional and decorative, the window's design and the surrounding brick pattern are the mason's trademark.

The summer kitchen is common to many ethnic groups, but the outdoor bake oven that shares a common gable wall with and is attached to the kitchen is distinctive. The oven was constructed on a platform of local dolomite, which stood four feet high and extended beyond the gable end of the summer kitchen. The oval, domed baking chamber was constructed of bricks made from local clays and rested on the platform. To protect the oven platform from weather damage, a frame gabled roof was built over the entire structure. Access to the oven exterior for repairs was through a door in the gable end; access to the baking chamber was through a small door inside the summer kitchen. As wood-fueled cook stoves gained in popularity, they tended to usurp the bake oven's function. The remaining ovens are cultural relics, used only during religious holidays.

Belgian roadside chapels are small structures situated near the road at the edge of the farmyard. Constructed as votive chapels by the devout Belgian Catholics, they were originally dedicated to various saints or the Blessed Virgin in gratitude for favors sought and received through prayer. Although the chapels may be used now for more general purposes, such as family devotions, their primary function

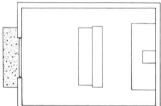

Chapel (1952), near Arlon, Belgium, distinguished by its arched, open entrance and use of stone and slate. (William G. Laatsch)

Left and below: Chapel (late 19th century), Door Peninsula, Wis. Typically frame, this American version has a sign that says, "Pray for us." (William G. Laatsch)

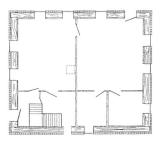

Above and right: John Baptist Massart House (c. 1872), Rosiere, Wis., a traditional brick-veneer Belgian-American house. Typically, the kitchen and parlor were the two largest rooms, and the smaller rooms were used as bedrooms. The parlor entrance was seldom used. (Heritage Hill Corporation; William G. Laatsch)

is to serve as a place of prayer for people seeking relief from afflictions. The rectangular chapels were typically nine feet long, seven and a half feet wide and about nine feet high at the peak of the gable. A large portion of the interior space was occupied by the altar, which held an assortment of religious artifacts. At most, four people could comfortably occupy a chapel.

Most commonly, the chapels were of frame construction, sided with either clapboards or composition shingles. Less frequently, local dolomite was used. Whether stone or frame, the chapels exhibit surprising internal uniformity. Inside walls and ceilings were finished with lath and plaster or wallboard, usually painted pale blue, green or yellow. Adorning the walls and reading like the pages of a family Bible were religious pictures and various birth, baptismal, first communion, marriage and death certificates.

Typically Belgian farmsteads exhibited a variety of structures reflecting changes in agricultural systems, practices and technology. The largest structure in the ensemble often was a dairy barn. The two most common types were the older gabled-roof, three-bay barn adapted for dairying and the basement barn, or dairy barn, with livestock housed on the ground floor. It usually had frame, masonry or log walls, and the frame upper level was a large hayloft. Long, low, log hay barns were also common. The logwork, in contrast to the three-bay barns and some of the other structures, was rough, and the unchinked gaps between the logs were wide to allow for the free passage of air. Logs were also used in horse barns, granaries, pig sties and smokehouses. Belgian farms are changing rapidly, however. Today, the progressive farmer has metal pole barns flanked by

Massart House with its brick veneer removed during dismantling before restoration, exposing the log structure. (William G. Laatsch)

expensive silos. Older log structures have been effectively adapted to new uses or destroyed.

Since the 1850s the Belgians on Wisconsin's southern Door Peninsula have created a cultural region with distinctive foods, traditions, values, institutions and architecture. The most distinctive element of Belgian architecture continues to be the brick house. These modest structures have, by and large, changed little over the last hundred years. As families expanded, a larger house was built or a mobile home was moved to the site. The summer kitchens and chapels are effective complements to the house. The barns, however, more strongly reflect economic progress rather than unique ethnic traditions. Undoubtedly the next 130 years will bring many changes to this distinctive landscape.

Belgian bake house (1774), an Old
World prototype. The oven is
attached to the gable end of the
summer kitchen. (Josef Weyns,
*Bakhuis en Broodbakken in
Vlaanderen*)

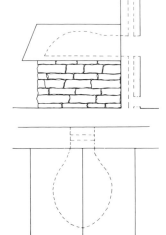

Right above and below: Section
and plan of a Belgian-American
bake oven. The oven's dimensions
(approximately 6 feet long, 4 feet
wide and 2 feet high) were uniform
to facilitate the baking process, in
which heat radiated from the oven
walls and floor. (William G.
Laatsch)

Traditional log Belgian barn on a
Belgian-American dairy farm,
Brown County, Wis. (William G.
Laatsch)

Bake oven, Door Peninsula, Wis., resting on a dolomite base. As in Belgium, it was attached to the gable end of the summer kitchen and covered by a small gabled roof. (William G. Laatsch)

CHINESE
Christopher Lee Yip

Because Chinese Americans have always made up a small portion of the U.S. population, their patterns of building have had little impact on American architecture as a whole, but Chinatown has become an important element in many American cities, from San Francisco to New York.

The first wave of Chinese immigration began with the California gold rush of 1849. The vast majority of Chinese immigrants came from Guangdong Province, located next to the British colony of Hong Kong and the Portuguese colony of Macau. Later, Chinese men came in search of labor in the Far West. Generally, they left their wives and children in their homeland in the hope of returning to China as soon as possible, with the intention of retiring in their native place. The passage of the Chinese exclusion acts beginning in 1882 also began limiting Chinese immigrants to men. As a result, the Chinese population of the United States remained overwhelmingly male throughout the 19th and 20th centuries.

Chinatowns tended to be composed of standard American commercial and tenement buildings altered to suit a male community — mainly multiple-storied commercial buildings containing residential hotels for single men as well as commercial and institutional spaces. They were usually located at the edge of the central business district, where cheap housing was available close to employment opportunities. During most of the 19th century little effort was made to make these buildings look like buildings in China because the structures, overall shapes, settings and social situations were so different in the United States. Shops would occupy the ground floors, with storage, club rooms and gambling establishments squeezed into the basements. Often, single residential hotel rooms with communal services along the corridors occupied the middle floors, while the top floor was used to house one of the important benevolent associations or a temple, as with the Tien How Temple (1852, 1906) in San Francisco's Chinatown.

Shops occupied the street frontages with grocers displaying their produce along the sidewalk. These shops usually had counters along one or both sides of the room and a small shrine at the back to help guarantee the owner prosperity and success. The shrine might consist of a small niche with an image of the deity, a container for incense

Opposite: Chinatown, San Francisco, in the 1890s. (Bancroft Library, University of California, Berkeley)

Interior of an art dealer's shop in San Francisco before 1906. (Special Collections, San Francisco Public Library)

Above: Joss House (1874), Weaverville, Calif., a temple erected by the local Chinese community at the time of the rush to find gold in the Trinity Alps of northern California. (Roger Sturtevant, HABS)

Main altar, Lung Gong Temple, San Francisco, an urban joss house photographed in 1887. (I.W. Taber, Bancroft Library, University of California, Berkeley)

Restaurant interior, San Francisco, seen before 1906, decorated in the elaborate Chinese baroque style. (I.W. Taber, Bancroft Library, University of California, Berkeley)

Left and below: Chinatown Telephone Exchange, San Francisco, about 1909, adapted from a freestanding pagoda, now a bank. (Christopher Yip; Special Collections, San Francisco Public Library)

and a few altar pieces placed on a table in front of the deity or only an image mounted on the wall. Chinese apothecaries had walls lined with small drawers, each containing a different herb, mineral or ingredient. Ailing customers would describe their problems to the herbalist, who would mix a combination of herbs to be taken. A large chopping block was a prominent feature of the shop.

The more lavishly decorated buildings were not residences but the fancy shops and community institutions such as temples and benevolent associations. These spaces tended to reflect the symmetrical, hierarchically organized layouts of Chinese traditions and used imported furniture and decoration.

Temples could be found in both urban and rural Chinatowns. Because Chinese religion was polytheistic, temples tended to have many gods and goddesses and multiple altars for prayers to the various deities. Generally, the primary deity was located on the main axis of the central room with lesser deities at flanking altars and in other rooms. An image of the deity would be flanked by retainers and lesser deities under a canopy placed behind an altar table with various vessels, including at least one for incense sticks. Carved and gilded wood surrounds and moldings and silk scrolls would be donated by worshipers and associations until temple interiors became quite elaborately decorated. One of the best-preserved rural temples, the Joss House (1849) in Weaverville, Calif., was erected at the time of the gold rush.

Most benevolent associations, made up only of males, based their membership on district, village, dialect or kinship bonds and functioned as social and quasi-political organs of the community. In large Chinatowns each association sought the most elaborate and prestigious building and often located its rooms on the top floor, whose facade would be decorated with balconies with lights, inscribed marble door surrounds and protective curving eaves above.

Discrimination in hiring forced many Chinese-Americans into the restaurant and laundry businesses. During the late 19th and early 20th centuries fancy restaurants would import carved scenes, wall decorations, lanterns, tables, chairs and decorative porcelain to furnish their

Opposite and below: Locke, Calif., a town of mostly simple wood structures built by Chinese in the early 20th century. The Jan Ying Association boasted a kitchen with space for many woks. (Both, Jet Lowe, HABS)

Chee Kung Tong Society Headquarters (early 20th century), Lahaina, Maui, Hawaii, an association building. (Jack E. Boucher, HABS)

Neon sign, Chinatown, San Francisco, combining Chinese images with a modern commercial approach. (Christopher Yip)

Yung See San Fong House (1916-17), Los Gatos, Calif., inspired by traditional Chinese architecture. (Matthew Poe, HABS)

Friendship Gate (1984), Chinatown, Philadelphia, a good example of the use of a traditional Chinese building form to express community identity and pride. (Philadelphia Convention and Visitors Bureau)

interiors. The elaborately carved screens from Guangdong and Hong Kong depicted historical, mythical, opera and religious scenes in the baroque fashion of South China.

Rural Chinatowns dotted the Far West as Chinese laborers began work in railroad construction, mining and agriculture, as in the Sacramento and San Joaquin valleys of California. The small agricultural Chinatowns of the late 19th and early 20th centuries, such as Locke, Calif., functioned as service centers for farm workers and were usually densely packed clusters of simple wood structures at the edge of a levee or farming community. A benevolent association building could usually be found among the boarding houses and commercial establishments.

During the early 20th century Chinatowns turned toward tourism, leading to a more conscious effort to present an exotic image. Neon signs made their appearance to advertise the businesses of the little Cathays. After World War II Chinatowns became symbols of an ethnic heritage, and gateways and other structures modeled on Chinese prototypes were erected as Chinese-Americans began moving to the suburbs.

CZECHS
David Murphy

The first Czechs to emigrate from east-central Europe —
ethnic *Čechs* from Bohemia and Moravia — were part of a
general Protestant exodus following the battle of White
Mountain near Prague in 1620. Thereafter, relatively small
numbers began arriving in North America, primarily in
New Amsterdam and the Delaware Valley, with Dutch and
Swedish trading companies, and then later with other
ethnic settlers from the German-Bohemian borderlands.
Larger migrations were stimulated by the Revolution of
1848. Following the passage of the Homestead Act of 1862
in the United States, Bohemians and Moravians began
arriving en masse. Of the estimated 400,000 who came to
America, nearly 87 percent arrived between 1848 and 1914.
By the end of the 19th century, just less than half of all
Czechs lived in New York, Chicago and Cleveland, while
most Czech farmers settled in Wisconsin, Iowa, Nebraska,
Minnesota and Texas. Other Czechs settled in Baltimore
and St. Louis and in Michigan, Missouri, Kansas and North
and South Dakota.

Czechs brought a variety of traditional construction
systems to the New World. They were one of the immigrant
groups credited with introducing log technology, characterized by chink wall construction, with the spaces between
the logs filled with wood staves, plastered with mud or lime
mortar. Minor outbuildings were often built with unhewn
beams, using square, saddle or V notches to secure the
corners. For most buildings, beams were planked on the
inside and outside faces, with half or full dovetail notches
used at the corners. Other common carpentry practices
included interior log partitions dovetailed to the exterior
walls, vertically mortised timber door and window jambs
and beamed loft floor structures. Simple common-rafter
roofs, with or without collar beams, predominate in
buildings constructed from all materials. Earthen struc-

Frank Nesbya Farm, Howard County, Neb., in the 1880s. The two-room
cottage at left replaced the house in ruins at center. (Nebraska State
Historical Society)

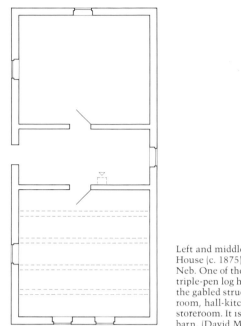

Left and middle: John Ružička House (c. 1875), Knox County, Neb. One of the best preserved triple-pen log houses in Nebraska, the gabled structure had a sitting room, hall-kitchen and chamber-storeroom. It is now used as a calf barn. (David Murphy)

Paider House (c. 1865), Kewaunee County, Wis. With the clapboarding removed, the characteristic full dovetail notching and filled chink walls are visible. (William H. Tishler)

Franz Zavadil House (c. 1885), Cedar County, Neb. Built by a noted Bohemian mason, the house displays fieldstone walls and chalk-rock quoins. (David Murphy)

tures in America used unfired clay brick, puddled clay and rammed earth. Masonry techniques included fired brick, a crude mud-mortared fieldstone method and the lime-mortared rubble stone wall.

The abundance of land in America and the Homestead Act requirement that farmers live on their own property led Czechs to adapt traditional building forms. Neither the rural Czech village arrangement, in which houses were typically oriented with the narrow, gable end facing the street or common, with the entrance off a narrow private courtyard, nor the compact farm courtyard was transplanted to America in the 19th century, although loosely arranged courtyard plans are evident. Building types, however, were retained largely intact, although built as detached structures modeled on attached predecessors.

Only a few of the numerous Czech house types were used in America. All had a single story, a narrow front gable wall and varying depth. Most popular were single-room cabins, two-room cottages and triple-pen houses, the smaller usually designed to be expanded into one of the larger types. The largest traditional house to be built in any number was a tripartite, central-passage house with spatial similarities to the northern European *parstuga* and the Anglo-American single-story central-passage house. Functionally, the *sín*, the narrow central hall in the Czech type, is not a through passage but a combination passage and work area (from which the ovens and stoves were fired) or a passage and kitchen. Nineteenth-century Czech-American examples were built with neither the large clay or masonry ovens, which were the primary functional rationale of the hall, nor the integral black kitchen, which had been

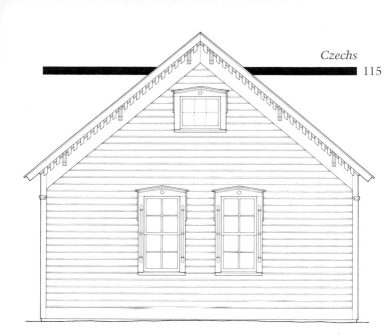

Tomek House (c. 1880), Knox County, Neb. This typically Bohemian-American facade recalls Old World versions through its brackets, pilasters and pedimented window hoods. (David Murphy)

Kounovsky House (1880s), Knox County, Neb. A variety of motifs in brick and wood on the front gable enhance the importance of the facade. (David Murphy)

abandoned before emigration. In America the preferred use was a combined hall-kitchen, which also housed the stair to the loft if there was one. Adjacent to the hall, on the street side, was the *světnice* (sitting room), the major living area, while on the opposite side was the *komora* (a smaller chamber), formerly a storage area but used in the New World primarily as a bedroom.

Another popular three-room type was the single-story, gabled, L-shaped house. Diminutive, shed-roofed ells were the most popular way of making modest additions to rectangular houses. A distinguishing feature of the ell types was the location of the kitchen (now a full-sized room) in the rear ell, while the sitting room retained its place in the front gabled section.

Numerous agricultural buildings were based on Old World types. Large three-bay log barns were built in Wisconsin, while smaller versions have been recorded in Nebraska and long narrow shed types in South Dakota. Smaller detached stables of log or frame construction were common, with stalls lined along the rear wall or placed along the end walls separated by a central aisle. A few examples of the cowshed or stable attached to the rear gable wall of the house in a familiar house-barn arrangement are extant.

The Czech-American house was related more in form than aesthetics to Old World models, although front-facing gables predominated. Ornamentation tended to be minimal but still focused on the *štít* (gable). The popularity of recessed porches, or porches attached to the side but fronting on the gable, also provided a location for ornament. The adoption of American clapboarding perhaps

Charvat House-Barn (1870s), relocated to Vancura Memorial Park, Tabor, S.D. A rare surviving house with attached cow shed, the clapboards have been removed. (John Rau, South Dakota Historical Preservation Center)

reduced the decorative possibilities somewhat, as did a desire for a less foreign appearance. Decorative parapeted gables were not built on houses here in spite of lasting intellectual ties to the homeland, where nationalistic sentiment was manifested in a neobaroque revival. Czech-American romanticism was freely expressed, however, in the halls of the Česko-Slovenský Podporující Spolek (Č.S.P.S.) and the Západní Česko Bratrské Jednoty (Z.Č.B.J.), both major freethinking fraternal and social organizations. Several distinctive halls, built during the latter 19th and early 20th centuries, incorporated neobaroque, or free, non-Anglo versions of Renaissance design in the gable facade. Wherever Czechs settled in the New World, their traditions of technical architectural skill and decorative exuberance created an important part of the American cultural landscape. ▦

John and Kate Merkwan House stone shed (1870s), Bon Homme County, S.D. A remnant of the Old World farm courtyard, this long, narrow building combined several functions including a storeroom, cow shed and stable. (Rolene Schliesman, South Dakota Historical Preservation Center)

Matej Hrbek Stable (c. 1886), Knox County, Neb. This detached log stable featured three horse stalls and exceptionally well crafted full dovetail notching. (David Murphy)

Jan Kollar Z.Č.B.J. Hall (1921), Pawnee County, Neb. Built of brick and clay tile and stuccoed, this has one of the finest neobaroque facades of any similar Czech-American hall. (David Murphy)

DANES
Thomas Carter

Danish emigration into the United States occurred primarily during the second half of the 19th century. Between
1850 and the outbreak of World War I, nearly 300,000
Danes — or one out of every 10 — came to the United
States. The emigration was, according to historian Kristian
Hvidt, "a factor in Danish history, most likely of greater
human and economic scope and consequence than all wars
or political crises." Against the backdrop of 19th-century
American history, however, the impact of Danish immigration seems negligible. Compared to other immigrant
groups, the Danes were few in number and often over-
shadowed by their more numerous Nordic neighbors, the
Swedes and Norwegians. So it has been also with Danish-
American architecture: While Scandinavian ethnic building traditions have figured prominently in recent vernacular architecture studies, the Danish contribution has
gone unnoticed. Fieldwork has just begun to define the
nature of Danish-American architecture.

A few Danish immigrants had found their way to
America by the 1820s and 1830s, but it was not until 1850
and the establishment of a successful Danish mission by
the Church of Jesus Christ of Latter-Day Saints, the
Mormons, that movement began in earnest. The first
Danish Mormons answered the call to Zion (Utah) in 1853,
and during the next 40 years nearly 13,000 made their way
to Mormon communities in the West. Few Utah towns
were without a Danish population, and several, such as
Ephraim and Mantua, were nearly all Danish. By the 1860s
the focus of Danish immigration had shifted to the upper
Midwest. There the Danes found land and opportunity, and
soon the areas around Elkhorn, Iowa, and Tyler, Minn.,
became strongholds of Danish culture in the American
heartland. In building their settlements, the Danes, like
other immigrants, often drew on their experience in the old
country.

Opposite and below: First floor of the Cornelius Jensen Ranch (1868–70),
Riverside, Calif., and the Danish home (c. 1850) of his relatives. The
ranch uses the Danish pattern of formal rooms across the front and
smaller ones to the rear. (Thomas Carter; County of Riverside Parks
Department)

Kronborg (1898), Tyler, Minn., built by Laurits and Anna Petersen and later demolished by an oil company. The raised first floor, hipped roof, segmentally arched windows and dormers recall Danish houses of a century before. (Courtesy John and Olga Opfell)

A Danish antecedent, Friboes Hvile (1756–58), Copenhagen Lyngby-Tarbaek. *(Danmarks Arkitektur)*

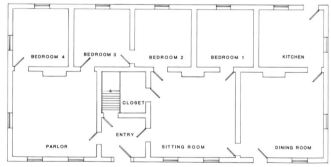

Andrew Petersen House (c. 1870–75), Richfield, Utah, one of many gabled masonry homes built by the Danes in Utah. Originally a three-room pair house, its bedrooms flanked a central kitchen–living area. (Thomas Carter)

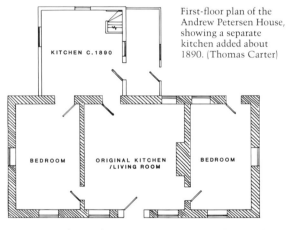

First-floor plan of the Andrew Petersen House, showing a separate kitchen added about 1890. (Thomas Carter)

KITCHEN C.1890

BEDROOM

ORIGINAL KITCHEN /LIVING ROOM

BEDROOM

Vernacular architecture in Denmark during the 17th and 18th centuries represented an extension of medieval practices. Houses were asymmetrical and of half-timber construction, had low-pitched thatched roofs and were of several types. In the east, the living room or hall and service rooms were arranged to either side of a small stove-kitchen; in the western districts, rooms were clustered around the hall, which contained an open fireplace and served as the kitchen. These regional house types persisted into the 1800s but by midcentury were increasingly being replaced in urban areas and on the more prosperous farms by new, classically inspired designs. The new architecture came in the form of a symmetrical detached house, built of masonry, with either thatch or tile roofing. Some regional variation continued in the house plan itself, yet most often a double-pile (two-room deep) arrangement was preferred. Although there are some signs of the persistence of older Danish building styles and techniques, more often it was the newer bourgeois architecture that was brought to America.

Several types of Danish-American houses exist. The largest has a complex double-pile plan. The stairway entrance hall and the more formal rooms — the parlor, living room and dining room — are located across the front, while a tier of smaller rooms containing sleeping chambers and the kitchen is located to the rear. Such houses were found throughout Denmark in the 19th century, although

Peter Schmidt House (c. 1900), Norway Township, S.D. Its hipped roof
and segmental hood molds over the windows tie it to earlier country
houses in Denmark. (South Dakota Historical Preservation Center)

Erik Simonsen House (1879), Audubon County, Iowa, a common Danish-
American house type characterized by a prominent central facade dormer.
(Signe T. Nelsen Betsinger)

the extent of their occurrence in the United States is not
fully known.

More common in Danish-American communities, although not in Denmark, was the three-room pair house,
characterized by a center room, usually the largest and
often used as a combination kitchen–living room, flanked
by a pair of smaller rooms to either side. The three rooms
are arranged axially under a gabled roof. Walls are usually of
masonry construction, and common-rafter roof framing is
typical. In Utah, adobe with heavy purlin framing was
widely used. The pair house appears as a scaled down, one-
room-deep version of a popular Danish *herrgard* (country
house) from the late 18th and early 19th centuries and was
found throughout the Mormon-settled West and the upper
Midwest during the second half of the 19th century.

Another common dwelling type in Danish-American
communities is the one-and-a-half-story, central passage
house with a centrally placed front wall dormer. Although
generally associated with Anglo-American folk building,
the central-passage house also surfaced in Denmark during
the 19th century and may in fact represent a type of pan–
northern European popular architecture of the period;
further research is needed to establish its Danish
connections.

Farm buildings and plans warrant similar research.
Several traditional farmstead types were found in Denmark,
although generally the house, barn and service buildings

Barn at Peter Schmidt's farm, Norway Township, S.D., a long, gabled-roof brick structure reminiscent of Danish barns during the period of emigration. (South Dakota Historical Preservation Center)

were arranged around an open yard. In Mormon communities where the farmstead consisted of a square city block within a gridiron town plan, there seems to be little suggestion of older Danish forms. In the Midwest, however, initial fieldwork has revealed several Danish farm sites that appear to be related to Old World plans. Equally interesting are several South Dakota Danish barns that are strikingly similar to the large barns seen on farms in Denmark during the emigration period.

Folk schools, the product of a Danish education reform movement, are found in several midwestern Danish towns. Although designed in American styles, the folk school is characteristically Danish and worthy of recognition, as are the Lutheran churches for which Danish-American communities are known. These church buildings are often designed in a variant of the High Victorian Gothic style, but several, like St. Peder's Lutheran Church (1919–21) in Nysted, Neb., display the square entrance tower and stepped gables of the Dutch style prominent in 15th- and 16th-century Danish church architecture.

Most examples of Danish-American architectural expression were found in the immigrant generation. Victorian-era styles and types generally became favored in America, and Danish-style buildings were discarded along with older classical forms during the late 19th century. The evidence from the first generation, however, must be viewed as a small but important part of the collective record of America's ethnic architecture. ▣

Opposite: Timber-framed stable (c. 1870) infilled with brick, Jens Meining House, Mt. Pleasant, Utah, incorporating building techniques from Denmark. (Peter Gross)

Nysted Danish-American Folk School, Nysted, Neb., one of a number of reform-movement schools built in midwestern Danish-American towns. (Nebraska State Historical Society)

St. Peder's Lutheran Church (1919–21), Nysted, Neb., a Danish-American building whose stepped gables and square tower reflect an ecclesiastical style popular in Denmark. (David Murphy)

FINNS
Matti Kaups

As members of New Sweden, the Swedish colony established on the lower Delaware River in 1638, the Finns
helped introduce horizontal cross-timber log construction
to North America. Somewhat later the Germans and the
Swiss also brought the technique to the middle colonies.
Finns as well as Russians built with logs in Alaska in the
1700s, and Finnish carpenters helped construct Fort Ross
(1821), the Russian outpost near San Francisco. Beginning
in 1864 Finnish immigrants settled in Michigan, Wisconsin and Minnesota, attracted by the availability of land and
employment in copper and iron mines and logging camps.
While the Finns also settled in the Rocky Mountain states,
the Pacific Northwest and to a lesser extent in New
England, they were concentrated primarily in the upper
Midwest.

The sparsely settled coniferous and mixed forest lands of
the area allowed these immigrants to use their vernacular
log building traditions. In Finland as well as in the United
States, pine and spruce were the preferred construction
timber. For houses, logs were ax hewn to a plank shape on
the sides, but for hay barns and woodsheds they were left
round. The buildings generally rested on stone foundations
composed of four glacial boulders sunk in pebble-lined beds
at each of the corners. In structures such as saunas, where
heat retention was important, the Finns employed the
2,000-year-old northern European log construction technique of building with green or partially dried softwoods. A
hand-forged *vara* was used to scribe the logs, which were
hollowed out with an ax so that each fit snugly with the log
below, requiring no chinking. In buildings in which heat
retention was desired, the full dovetail or vertical double
notch was used. Other buildings were constructed with
saddle notches. Except for hay barns and woodsheds
constructed with round logs, the walls in other buildings
were generally of ax-hewn, plank-shaped logs on both
interior and exterior surfaces.

House in northern Finland in
1867. This one-and-a-half-story
house had plank-shaped wall logs
with vertical double notching and
birch-bark roofing held in place by
poles joined at the ridge. A
rainhood covered the doorway
leading to the central entrance
hall. The house was unpainted
except for the window frames and
had eyebrow windows rarely found
in Finnish-American examples.
(J. A. Friis, National Museum of
Finland)

The houses Finnish immigrants built in the United States were essentially continuations of five basic types constructed in Finland in the 19th century, although smaller and less pretentious. The smallest was a one-story, one-room, nearly square house. The two-room house was most common. The front door led to the kitchen, which also functioned as a living room and bedroom, while the other room served as an unheated parlor–visitor's room. However, if the family was large the parlor could serve as a combination living room–bedroom. The house could be enlarged by the addition of another room of equal size to form an elongated I shape or an L or T shape. The one-story, rectangular Nordic pair dwelling had a tripartite layout, a central entrance hall and two rooms. The one-and-a-half-story house had various floor plans — a bisected rectangular design, a bi- or trisected L- or T-shaped layout, or square. These houses differed considerably in size and had either two or three rooms on the first floor. Eyebrow windows, a distinguishing feature of one-and-a-half-story houses in Finland, were far less common in houses constructed by immigrants. Only a few two-story houses with a rectangular or square layout were built. Most of the larger one-and-a-half- and two-story houses were constructed after the initial settlement phase. Significantly, the large two-story houses of affluent farmers in Finland had no counterparts in Finnish settlements in America.

The Finns' houses had certain basic elements in common: They were freestanding single-family units that lacked indoor plumbing, basements and bathing facilities. The plank-shaped wall logs were not painted. The exteriors of some were in time sided with tar paper or boards and painted. Initially the inside walls were left in a natural state but later were partially wainscoted or covered with newsprint, wallpaper or pressed paper boards. Manufactured doors and double-hung windows were used from the early years of settlement. Unless houses were equipped with rainhoods, the doorways were protected with open or enclosed frame porches; the latter functioned as storage for outdoor clothing and served as pantries, sometimes parti-

Below and center: Nordic pair house (c.1910), St. Louis County, Minn., with vertical siding covering horizontal logs. The three-room plan was modified by the addition of an enclosed porch. (Both, Matti Kaups)

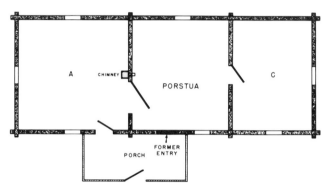

Plan of a one-story, two-room house, the most common form built by Finnish immigrants. The parlor was at left and the kitchen at right. (Matti Kaups)

Finnish house in Minnesota, with a pig sty in the foreground. The rectangular two-room dwelling has birch-bark roofing. Both structures used plank-shaped walls and vertical double notching. (Matti Kaups)

tioned. Some early houses had stovepipe chimneys, but brick was more commonly used. The chimneys generally occupied a central location, although in some houses they were situated along a side or gable wall. The lofts, and in larger houses the upper floors, were usually only partially completed, if at all, and served as storage space and as supplemental sleeping quarters during warm weather. The prevalent roof type in all structures was the saddle or gabled roof. This was covered with shingles, tar paper and sometimes hollowed logs (a scoop roof), overlapping boards and sheets of birch bark held in place by cedar roof poles joined at the ridge. In the early years of settlement thatch was used as roofing on some hay and cow barns.

The grouping of outbuildings (also mostly log) on Finnish farmsteads generally followed an L-shaped or nearly square pattern. There were many variations, however, ranging from random placement to linear patterns and reflecting economics, the U.S. Rectangular Land Survey, local topography and Finnish regional traditions. The sauna was a ubiquitous feature on every farm. Chimneyless until the 1920s, it was considered a fire hazard and was located away from the farmstead proper. Besides being a bathhouse, it was the farm clinic in which children were born, people were healed, laundry was washed, small amounts of grain were dried, malt was made, and meat and fish cured. Other outbuildings (all log and unpainted) included storehouse-granaries and a *riihi* (a barn for drying and threshing grain). Ravaged by time, some of these structures are still standing on the landscape.

The vernacular architecture of Finnish immigrants, most of whom came relatively late to the United States and lived in ethnic enclaves, had no immediate impact on American architecture. Since then, however, an aesthetic appreciation has evolved for the craftsmanship evident in the carefully fashioned Finnish log structures and for the sauna, the Finns' important contribution to American culture. ▨

House of Finnish immigrants in Wisconsin about 1890. The one-and-a-half-story L-shaped home was built with dovetail notching, a shingle roof, open porch and double-hung windows. A well sweep is at right.

Minnesota tripartite barn for livestock (left), pigs and sheep (center) and hay (right) of horizontal and vertical logs. (Matti Kaups)

Minnesota field hay barn with inward-sloping walls, saddle notching and ventilation space between the logs. (Matti Kaups)

Right: *Vara* used to scribe logs. (Matti Kaups)

Unmortared fieldstones used to build a sauna stove. (Matti Kaups)

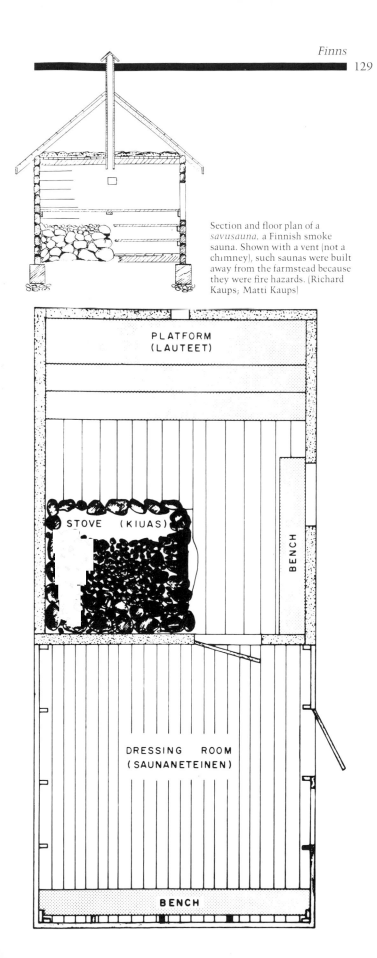

Section and floor plan of a *savusauna,* a Finnish smoke sauna. Shown with a vent (not a chimney), such saunas were built away from the farmstead because they were fire hazards. (Richard Kaups; Matti Kaups)

PLATFORM
(LAUTEET)

STOVE (KIUAS)

BENCH

DRESSING ROOM
(SAUNANETEINEN)

BENCH

GERMAN-RUSSIANS
Michael Koop

German-Russian folk buildings represent an unusual synthesis of central European and Russian-Ukrainian architectural features. The migration of several hundred thousand Germans to western Russia during the mid-18th and early 19th centuries led to an integration of their house form with native Russian construction techniques and the creation of a distinctive building type. In the early 1870s two German-Russian subgroups began emigrating to America: The Volga Germans settled primarily in Kansas and Nebraska, and the Black Sea Germans located in North and South Dakota. Members of both groups, particularly Mennonites, later settled in the western Canadian provinces of Alberta, Manitoba and Saskatchewan. Unlike many other ethnic cultures, German-Russians were accustomed to the harsh environment and relatively flat, treeless Great Plains landscape, which topographically is similar to the steppes of western Russia. Using indigenous resources in a region notorious for inadequate building materials, the settlers erected sturdy clay and stone residences, churches and outbuildings in both rural and urban areas.

These buildings were not the ephemeral sod structures commonly associated with Great Plains settlement; rather, skillful German-Russian builders used a material composed of clay mixed with manure, straw and water. This combination produced a durable substance naturally suited to the prairie landscape. Two techniques were used for constructing load-bearing walls: puddled clay, in which clay

Peter Barkman House-Barn (1880), Hillsboro, Kans., constructed entirely of puddled clay. The barn section is on the right. (Kansas State Historical Society)

was layered on a stone foundation, and rammed earth, in which an earthen mixture was compacted between wooden forms. One variation of the puddled clay wall used medium-sized stones regularly placed in the lower part of the wall. Another use of clay involved pressing adobelike bricks out of wooden molds, known locally as *Batsa.* German-Russians eventually combined *Batsa* brick with balloon-frame construction, placing clay brick in walls between vertical studs to stabilize and insulate the dwelling. Clay also functioned as a mortar in masonry walls; it was shaped into large biscuits or blocks or used as a protective coating on interior and exterior wall surfaces. No fewer than 11 construction techniques involving clay developed in South Dakota.

Both the Volga and Black Sea German-Russians introduced to the Great Plains similar yet distinct house forms that were common to their Russian homeland but likely had their roots in central Europe. Each house type was typically one story high with a loft and had a *Vörhausl* (attached vestibule) leading into the kitchen. Volga German-Russian houses usually had hipped roofs and were slightly longer than wide, with the entrance located along the facade close to the gable end. By contrast, Black Sea German-Russian houses were generally larger than those in Volga settlements and had a rectangular shape with a gabled roof. House-barn combinations, which provided living quarters for people and animals under a single roof,

Plan of the Ludwig Deckert House (c. 1879), Hutchinson County, S.D., a typical two-bay German-Russian house with a central furnace – bake oven. The gable-end entrance, a later addition, is unusual. (Michael Koop)

were also common among Black Sea builders; ancillary farm structures included barns, sheds and root cellars.

Rooms were subdivided by puddled clay and *Batsa* brick partitions, creating a house two or three bays wide and one or two rooms deep. A central kitchen was typically flanked to the left by a parlor–living room and sometimes a storage or sleeping room on the right. Some houses had a *schwarze Küche* (black kitchen), a small, centrally located, six-foot-square room separated by *Batsa* that functioned as a separate space for preparing and cooking food. Abutting the black kitchen and heating the parlor and rear bedroom was a device distinctive to German-Russians: a furnace–bake oven, commonly referred to as a Russian oven or Mennonite stove. The spatial arrangement of the *schwarze Küche* and furnace–bake oven is not uncommon to many regions in central Europe; this form was transplanted through western Russia to several settlement areas in the Great Plains. An unusual use of clay was demonstrated in the loft, where massive interior chimneys, up to 15 feet high and of various shapes, were fashioned of puddled clay, *Batsa* or large clay blocks.

Calcimine mixed with coloring agents produced bright blue, olive green, brown and mustard yellow colors that, when applied with a brush, rag, sponge or even a corncob, traditionally covered ceilings, walls, floors, framed doorways and windows. Decorative stencils were occasionally traced along the cornice near the ceiling.

As commercially produced and distributed building materials and instruction manuals became more common during the first quarter of the 20th century, German-Russians gradually abandoned their folk architectural tradition in favor of mainstream American building practices. Many distinctive ethnic features such as the early clay construction methods, furnace – bake oven and decorative paint schemes have been removed or obscured through interior and exterior modernizations. Despite these changes, German-Russian buildings are the richest and most significant collection of vernacular architecture in the northern Plains, harmoniously blending into the landscape. ▨

Log house with a thatched roof (mid-19th century), built by a German-Russian in Volhynia, Russia, a heavily forested area. (American Historical Society of Germans from Russia)

Catholic church (1895), Campbell County, S.D., built of *Batsa* brick on a stone foundation. (Assumption Abbey Archives, Hebron, N.D.)

Left: Oven made of rocks and *Batsa* brick, George Vetter House (c. 1878), Hutchinson County, S.D. A hinged metal door once covered the opening. (South Dakota Historical Preservation Center)

Frank Hutmacher House (1928), Dunn County, N.D., a stone and puddled clay house. The roof of logs, branches and straw sealed with clay was common earlier but unusual on such a late structure. (State Historical Society of North Dakota)

George Lismann House (c. 1909), Lincoln, Neb., now a church, a one-story, four-square, hipped-roof house typical of Volga German-Russian houses. (Janet Spencer, Nebraska State Historical Society)

Rammed-earth, load-bearing walls, Vetter House, formed by tiers of clay three feet high rammed between wood braces. (South Dakota Historical Preservation Center)

Two-foot-thick walls, Gottlieb Stern House (c. 1885), Hutchinson County, S.D., a common German-Russian means of insulation. Angled windows helped capture additional heat and light. (South Dakota Historical Preservation Center)

Fleur-de-lys stenciled frieze, Henry Mayer House (1878), Hutchinson County, S.D., one form of decoration used by German-Russians in their houses. (South Dakota Historical Preservation Center)

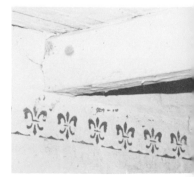

Johann Rempfer House (late 19th century), Yankton County, S.D., an
archetypal three-bay German-Russian house built of frame and *Batsa*
brick with a *Vörhausl.* (South Dakota Historical Preservation Center)

Plan of the Rempfer House
showing the *Batsa* infill between
the wall studs and a second
Vörhausl on the rear facade.
(Michael Koop)

JAPANESE
Ronald K. K. Lee

Because the architecture of Japan directly inspired some of the pioneers of modern architecture, its influence on Japanese-American buildings is a complex matter to sort out. Commercial and cultural exchange across the Pacific beginning with Commodore Matthew Perry's voyage to Yokohama in 1853 brought the world of Japanese art to America. Japanese architecture became known to Americans through ukiyoe prints, books and a number of authentically designed buildings constructed for American expositions, the most significant of which was the Japanese exhibit at the World's Columbian Exposition in Chicago in 1893. This wood building by the Japanese architect Masamichi Kura remained standing on its wooded site until it was destroyed by fire in 1946, outlasting the neoclassical buildings of the exposition. It must surely have been studied by architects of the Prairie School and was certainly seen by Frank Lloyd Wright, who was working for Louis Sullivan at the time.

The characteristics of Japanese houses were first described for Westerners by Edward S. Morse in his book *Japanese Homes and Their Surroundings* (1885). Morse, an American zoologist, studied houses in Japan in the 1870s and noted that they had no doors or windows in the familiar Western sense but, instead, movable screens in place of walls. This was possible, he reported, because rather than being an enclosure of load-bearing walls, the house had a wood structural frame. Exterior materials — wood, tile and plaster — were all left in their natural state. The basis of Japanese architecture was respect for nature and for the nature of materials. Architecture and nature were one and the same. Frank Lloyd Wright's concept of

Japanese exhibit on a wooded island at the World's Columbian Exposition in Chicago, 1893. The oriental setting was created in a sea of Classical Revival buildings. (Witteman, *The World's Fair, Chicago, 1893,* 1898)

continuous interior spaces that flowed out into the land-scape, his respect for the nature of materials and his belief that buildings should be designed with nature — all have parallels in Japanese architecture.

In 1880 there were 145 Japanese in America. By 1900 the number had risen to 85,437, and in 1980 the Japanese population numbered 716,331. Japanese were reported in the kingdom of Hawaii as early as 1868, and from territorial days the Japanese have constituted a major percentage of the population of the Hawaiian islands. Hawaii today is rich with examples of Japanese-inspired architecture.

The Japanese immigrants who chose to live in America quickly adopted local habits, and the first buildings were built in the local manner. In Hawaii they used single-wall wood framing, known locally as the Hawaiian plantation style. The Ewa Japanese Club at Ewa Plantation on Oahu is an example that dates from the 1920s.

The Maui Jinsha Mission (1915), a Shinto shrine on Maui, is an early example of a blend of plantation style and traditional Shinto architecture. Japanese shrine carpenters Seichi Tomokiyo and Ichitaro Takata were brought from Japan to construct the traditional details with wood joinery. To this day, Shinto shrines such as the Kotohira Jinsha (1924) are renewed in traditional fashion with carpenters and materials brought in from Japan.

Buddhist congregations have taken a more international approach in the design of their temples, adopting the Christian practice of holding Sunday services and even seating the congregation in American-style pews. While some temples, such as the Shingon Temple (1917), were built in traditional Japanese style, others, such as the

Honpa Hongwanji Mission (1918, Emory and Webb) and the Soto Zen Mission (1953, Robert T. Katsuyoshi) were inspired by the architecture of India, reaching back beyond Japan to the source of Buddhism. In embracing an international approach, Japanese-American Buddhists express a global consciousness broader than the island nation from which they came and the island state in which they live.

An exceptional Christian building of note is the Makiki Christian Church (1932, Hego Fuchino), which was modeled on a Japanese castle. For the pastor and founder of the church, the Reverend Takie Okumura, this building symbolized refuge, security and grandeur, appropriate qualities for a Christian edifice.

The citizens of the 50th state live in Western-style houses; however, Hawaii has its share of Japanese-inspired domestic architecture. The Nellie Pew House (1930, Hart Wood) is noted for its free combination of Japanese, Chinese and Mediterranean decorative motifs, appropriate to Hawaii's multiracial community. The Alice Poole House (1931, Claude Stiehl) is Japanese-inspired; however, the use of native lava rock and the projecting screened porch at the upper level make this house seem perfectly suited for its Hawaiian hillside location. The Earl Ernst House (1950, Wimberly and Cook) is a faithful rendition of a traditional Japanese house, demonstrating how well suited this form is for Hawaii's benign climate.

The Japanese pitched-roof dwelling on a raised platform is an ancient southeast Asian building type still prevalent in the region today. After more than a hundred years of cultural assimilation, it is not easy to identify the resultant architecture as either Japanese or American. If this house type is constructed of modern materials and abstracted as a roofed platform in a garden, it is a contemporary Hawaiian house type with which many Pacific peoples can identify. John Hara's award-winning Kuliouou House (1984), for example, has been described as a contemporary Japanese residence, but the architect prefers to refer to it simply as a contemporary residence in Hawaii. It remains to be seen whether this building type will become a Pan-Pacific regional style of architecture. ▧

Ewa Japanese Club, Ewa, Oahu, a building from the 1920s showing the adoption of the Hawaiian plantation style. (Augie Salbosa)

Izumo Taishakyo Mission (1923, Hego Fuchino), Oahu, Hawaii, a traditional Shinto shrine. (Nancy Bannick)

Maui Jinsha Mission (1915, Seichi Tomokiyo and Ichitaro Takata), Wailuku, Maui. The building is an early melding of the plantation and Shinto styles of Hawaii and Japan. (Rick Regan)

Makiki Christian Church (1932, Hego Fuchino), Honolulu, an outstanding building based on a Japanese castle and symbolizing refuge, security and grandeur. (Augie Salbosa)

Alice Poole House (1931, Claude Stiehl), Honolulu, combining Japanese wood construction with Hawaiian lava rock. (Augie Salbosa)

Opposite: Nellie Pew House (1930, Hart Wood), Honolulu, which draws from Japanese, Chinese and Mediterranean motifs. (DLNR, Honolulu)

Kotohira Jinsha (1924), Honolulu, a Shinto shrine renewed following Japanese traditions, most recently by Tom Agawa in 1983. (Dwight Okumoto)

Honpa Hongwanji Mission (1918, Emory and Webb), Honolulu, a Buddhist temple with roots in India. (Nancy Bannick)

Earl Ernst House (1950, Wimberly and Cook), Honolulu, using traditional Japanese openings, screens and a rock garden. (Robert Wenkam)

MIDWESTERN GERMANS
William H. Tishler

During the 19th century, massive waves of Germans poured into the Midwest, which soon had the nation's greatest regional concentration of German-born Americans. Attracted to farming as a way of life on the frontier, they were established in southern Ohio by 1830. During the next decade, they had moved westward to areas around the Great Lakes and along the Ohio and Mississippi rivers. Here, colonies of immigrants settled in communities that often took on a distinctive German character. In the countryside, thousands of farmers and craftsmen bought up expansive tracts of farmland. With a strong love for the soil, they regarded their new land with a deep sense of permanency. Stability and longevity became hallmarks of their built environment and land ethic.

With many regional differences in history, dialect, religion and architecture in their homeland, German settlers brought diverse building skills and traditions to the Midwest. In their larger, more homogeneous enclaves, they perpetuated architectural forms, materials and construction methods that reflected customary Old World building patterns. Elsewhere, German carpenters and joiners, influenced by local environmental conditions and their new American neighbors, adopted prevailing styles, room arrangements and decorative embellishments. Thus, unlike the folk buildings of many other European ethnic groups in America's heartland, German-American vernacular architecture varied extensively.

Temporary log shelters frequently were built as the Germans' first houses and outbuildings. As survival and some degree of prosperity became more assured, the settlers' thoughts turned toward a more substantial house and other permanent structures, which could incorporate a wide range of construction systems and building materials. Brick and stone construction, familiar to the immigrants from nearly every province in Germany, was frequently used in larger structures such as churches, mills, breweries and gymnastic halls. Traditional half-timber structures were built by settlers from northern and eastern Germany. Log construction, predominant in the more abundantly wooded areas of southern and western Germany, continued where suitable timber was available, particularly in the

Opposite: Ella and Ida Scholz-Langholf in front of their *Fachwerk* (half-timber) house, near Watertown, Wis., about 1910. (Alex Krueger, State Historical Society of Wisconsin)

Right: *Fachwerk* construction detail of a Dodge County, Wis., house built about 1850. (William H. Tishler)

Fachwerk house (c. 1850) now located at Old World Wisconsin, Eagle, Wis., a large outdoor ethnic museum village. (William H. Tishler)

coniferous forests of the upper Great Lakes. The latter varied considerably in form throughout the Midwest, with two-, three- and four-room arrangements prevailing within a simple rectangular log shell. Because many German settlers came from cities or areas where timber was in short supply, they often were unskilled at log building. Thus, their structures frequently lacked the craftsmanlike refinements — precise corner joinery and log walls with minimal chinking — more commonplace in settlements of Nordic, Baltic and some eastern European ethnic groups.

The most distinctive of their midwestern building traditions were the half-timber, or *Fachwerk*, structures. This method of construction incorporated a sturdy, mortise-and-tenon framework of heavy, braced timbers nogged with clay or brick to form a continuous wall. Clusters of these buildings also were built outside the Midwest, at settlements in Texas, Pennsylvania and North Carolina. But by far the largest and best-known concentration can be found in Wisconsin, which attracted immigrants primarily from Pomerania, Brandenburg, Saxony and adjacent Prussian districts. Their home region of Germany, its forests depleted from warfare and intensive agriculture, had developed *Fachwerk* construction technology in response to prevailing wood shortages. Yet, in spite of Wisconsin's almost unlimited supply of timber, these German builders continued to favor this method throughout the east-central portion of the state. Called *deutscher Verband* in the local vernacular, it was used in the construction of houses, churches and farm buildings.

Early German farmstead with outbuildings and a *Fachwerk* house
arranged around an open courtyard
at Old World Wisconsin. (William
H. Tishler)

Rare 19th-century *Fachwerk*
house-barn, Dodge County, Wis.
The house is to the right; animals
and the harvest were sheltered in
the larger space at left. (William H.
Tishler)

Stone house-barn built by German-Americans in Dodge County, Wis.,
another rare 19th-century survivor. Animals were at left, with the living
quarters at right. (William H. Tishler)

Pelster House-Barn, Franklin County, Mo., a large frame structure with a porch and stone foundation, about 1900. The Pelster family is out front. (Missouri Cultural Heritage Center)

One of the most common forms of Old World peasant shelter — the house-barn — was almost totally rejected by European immigrants on their arrival in America. Yet, several remarkable examples, with *Fachwerk*, stone, brick and earthen walls, can still be found in rural German settlements. This unusual agrarian building sheltered humans, livestock and the harvest under a single roof. Generally a large, rectangular structure, it contained a house unit, with separate outside access, sharing a common wall with the larger barn area where cattle, poultry, crops and machinery were stored. Today, isolated house-barns survive in Wisconsin, the Dakotas and Missouri. Typically, however, early German farmsteads consisted of many separate structures for living, food processing (including their characteristic smokehouse) and livestock and crop storage functions. These were sometimes arranged in a *Vierseithof* (spacious, open-cornered courtyard).

Important concentrations of structures were built in German utopian settlements such as New Harmony, Ind., and the Amana Colonies in Iowa. The former, founded by the Rappites in 1815, incorporated ingenious construction features in their brick and half-timber buildings. These included prefabrication techniques for mass-producing standardized houses and innovations in insulation, foundation design and heating systems. At the Amanas, which began in 1855, settlements reflected the layout of medieval European agrarian villages. Located on high ground, they incorporated unadorned communal residences and artisan shops around a centrally located church and were dominated by barns and other agricultural buildings. Each colony was surrounded by rich agricultural land, creating a spacious rural environment that prevails to this day.

Much of the rich folk culture the Germans brought to this country began to decline after the turn of the 20th century. After two world wars, they became among the least visible of American ethnic groups. Yet, their achievements and contributions had a decided influence on the quality of life in the Midwest, and their vernacular architecture remains the purest and most visible component of this legacy. ▨

Below: Amana Colonies, Iowa, in the early 1900s. Kitchen gardens in the German utopian settlement were planted to surround houses and other structures in one of the villages. (Joan Liffring-Zug Collection)

Opposite: J. P. Tatsch House (1856), Fredericksburg, Tex. Similar to many limestone houses built by Texas Germans, this massive structure has an enormous chimney serving the kitchen. (Dell Upton)

Stone smokehouse and bake oven on an early German farmstead, Dodge County, Wis. (William H. Tishler)

Hans Haugan House (c. 1859),
Winneshiek County, Iowa. This
one-room Norwegian-American
log house with an entrance in the
gable end appears to be a direct
descendant of medieval examples
in Norway. (Darrell D. Henning)

Above: Medieval house type in
Telemark, Norway, with a gable-
end entrance and projecting roof
overhang. (Darrell D. Henning)

NORWEGIANS
Darrell D. Henning

From the isolated fjords and valleys of Norway, each with its own customs and traditions, more than 700,000 immigrants settled in America from 1825 to 1925. Only Ireland, of all the European countries, offered up a greater percentage of its citizens to America than did Norway. Most Norwegian immigrants came from the countryside and sought cheap land on the frontier as it expanded westward from Wisconsin to the Great Plains and Texas, the West Coast, Alaska and Hawaii. They brought with them a deeply rooted sense of tradition, reflected in the built environment wherever Norwegian settlements are found but most evident in the Midwest.

In Norway, log construction with regional variations was dominant at the time of emigration. In the New World, farmers kept preferred building forms but had little first-hand knowledge of construction, possibly because building had become a socialized trade in Norway. Norwegian log house construction was characterized by a long groove between the logs that formed tighter joints along the length of the log as the building settled; a double-cat notch (resembling Lincoln logs) to join the corners of the timbers was typical. While occasionally found in the New World, the long groove and grooved notch were used less often than dovetail corner joints with gaps between the logs filled with mortar. Early immigrants often constructed their first buildings with the sod roof so well adapted to the Norwegian climate, heavy ridge pole, purlins and relatively low pitch of Norwegian tradition. Eventually, roofing materials changed from sod to wood shingles and all buildings were

Below: Sjur Helgeland House (c. 1860), Worth County, Iowa, about 1911. In this popular *Akershusisk* plan house, the nearly centered door lends a more symmetrical appearance to the medieval form. (Vesterheim Museum)

constructed with American climate and materials in mind.

Immigrant house forms were often more faithful to their Old World models than were construction methods. Two house types were commonly used. A single-room, one-and-a-half-story structure appears to have been the preferred first permanent dwelling. The building was a gabled-roof, rectangular structure with a door and window near the center of the side wall. The plan usually included a stair to the loft on the other side of the door. A cast-iron cooking stove occupied the corner opposite the stair. Eventually these small dwellings were expanded with lean-tos at the rear or incorporated into larger structures. Often the simple homes served first-generation immigrants throughout their lives, and the succeeding generation built new, larger and sometimes less traditional homes.

The most typical Norwegian-style house still much in evidence is the two- and three-room dwelling. It is derived from the most ancient house form, from the Middle Ages, a one-room house, nearly square in plan, with a room of frame construction smaller by half on the gable end and a second floor often built entirely of logs. In the fully developed three-room plan, the smaller end of the house was divided, creating a *forstue* (separate entryway) and *kleve* (storeroom), both with access to the *stue* (main room). In the 18th century a house with a more symmetrical appearance became fashionable. This *Akershusisk* plan from the medieval house is the most common form associated with Norwegian-American farmsteads.

Expansion of Norwegian-American houses differed considerably from Old World practices. In Norway, a second *stue* typically was added to the end of the house with the smaller room or rooms, with the second *stue* functioning as a formal parlor. In America, a typical addition would be a T- or L-shaped kitchen at the back of the house, the former *stue* becoming a parlor or dining room. Only rarely was the house extended in linear Norwegian fashion.

Another Norwegian feature on the American landscape is the Norwegian version of the northern European bank barn. Built into a hill or bank, the lower level of the structure was of stone, logs or a combination of the two and

Medieval Norwegian house type with an enclosed entry *(forstue)*. The form is similar to the workman's house in Norway and the Forde House in Iowa, both seen below. (Dana Jackson)

Workman's house (mid-19th century), Gudbrandsdal, Norway, built in the typical frame and log, gabled-roof style. (Darrell D. Henning)

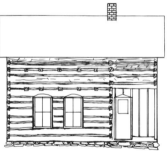

Forde House, Winneshiek County, Iowa, a two-room Norwegian-American home with a cantilevered forebay. (Darrell D. Henning)

Norwegian immigrant parsonage (c. 1870) in North Dakota. The eclectically patched roof illustrates an attempt — and the result — at sod-roof construction. (Vesterheim Museum)

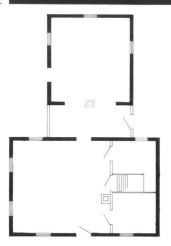

Left and below: Engum House (1888), Coon Valley, Wis., a second-generation Norwegian-American home seen about 1915. Similar in plan to the Helgeland House, this farmhouse has a full second floor and American-style porch. The small room at the top of the plan was an older one-room house later attached and used as a kitchen. (Brian Olsen; Norskedalen Museum)

housed the livestock. The upper portion, for hay storage, was usually built using post-and-beam construction. Entrance was gained by a ramp and bridge, which led to a level wide enough only for a team and wagon, between the hay floor and roof. A separate roof, either shed or gable type, was added to facilitate entrance at this level. Often the roof and walls were extended to enclose the bridge leading to the wagon floor.

The Norwegian-American farmstead was often laid out according to Old World patterns. Both the formal, rectangular plans of the broad valleys of eastern Norway and the linear or paired linear forms of the more rugged terrain are discernible in America. In the paired linear plan, the farm lane often divided the house, summer kitchen, well and shops on the up-slope side of the lane and the barn and other livestock buildings on the down-slope side.

Norwegian farmers immigrating to America's Midwest initially avoided the prairies, preferring to make their homes on wooded hills near a stream. Although initial building efforts often resembled Norwegian examples, immigrants were quick to adopt American customs such as wood shingled roofs, lapped siding, double-hung window sash and other conveniences offered for sale in the nearest town. American methods of farming were quickly adopted, thus affecting the size and character of the outbuildings. But the essence of Norway remained — a hillside location, a traditional house with white-painted siding or a particular approach and relationship between the house and barn. All helped to create a unifying character that breathed, "Ja, nu er vi hjemme" — "Ah, yes, we are home now."

Kittelson Barn (late 19th century), Winneshiek County, Iowa, a good example of a traditional Norwegian bank barn. Its gabled covered bridge leads to the central level of the haymow. (Darrell D. Henning)

David Thoe Barn, Telemark, Norway, a bank barn with a ramp leading to the central part of the haymow. The shed roof over the entrance indicates a raised section in the top log. (Darrell D. Henning)

Section through the Kittelson Barn, showing its framing and various levels. (Darrell D. Henning)

Olsen Barn, Nora Springs, Iowa, an adaptation to existing conditions. The massive ramp leading to the haymow compensates for the absence of natural Norwegian land forms. (Darrell D. Henning)

SWEDES
Lena A:son Palmqvist

"First build a house! They went out in the woods and picked out good sturdy trees. There were no sod houses or dugouts here, this being a thickly wooded area." As this late 19th-century settler in Minnesota succinctly observed, even early Swedish buildings were well adapted to the American environment.

Wood was the traditional building material of vernacular architecture in Sweden, and with wood came characteristic Swedish corner timbering techniques. The New Sweden settlement (1638 – 56) in the Delaware River Valley (extending from northern Delaware to southeastern Pennsylvania and southwestern New Jersey) bears evidence of Scandinavian corner timbering, probably introduced into what is now the United States at that time, as well as common Swedish house types. But the mass emigration from Sweden starting in the 1840s and culminating late in the century introduced other traditions. Although this was a period of beginning industrialization in Sweden, the majority of Swedish emigrants moved directly from the countryside to the United States — primarily the Delaware River Valley, Minnesota and Wisconsin — without ever having encountered the effects of Swedish industrialization.

The settlers brought with them the knowledge and often the tools to continue Swedish rural building traditions, such as log houses and barns, but they also chose other alternatives. Economic reality for the majority of them meant that their first dwelling in the new country had to be built at minimum cost using available local materials with labor provided by family or friends. That would seem to have ensured continuation of old building methods, at least in wooded areas. But the majority of the early log cabins were rather crude, often temporary structures, built rapidly to house the family during the first winter. These cabins and other early log buildings had a rectangular floor plan and were sometimes divided into two rooms, like Swedish single-room cottages with a small entrance hall; they also

Swedish settlers in front of a typical log cabin, Rush City, Minn., in 1887. (Nordiska Museet, Stockholm)

might have a small storage room and a *stuga* (an all-purpose room with a corner fireplace). The length of the logs determined the size of the building. These houses generally were built with traditional corner timbering to notch the logs but usually mixed different kinds of wood; mortar often was used as filling when the logs were uneven, even though it was not common in Sweden.

The *enkelstuga* (single-pen or one-room cottage), consisting of one unpartitioned, rectangular room, was a typical Swedish home from medieval times to the 1800s and was found along the lower Delaware Valley. The Swedes and the Finns in the valley were also familiar with a northern European house type, in Sweden known as a *parstuga* (a pair or two-room cottage with a wide hall flanked by chimneys). The American saddlebag house, with two rooms and a central chimney, is probably derived from the Swedish *stuga av celltyp* (cell-type cottage). Both Swedish and American saddlebag houses have two front doors, a shed porch and two rooms of approximately equal size. The Fenno-Scandinavian gatehouse, known in Sweden as a *portlider,* is quite similar to the dogtrot house of the Delaware area. Mansions built in Sweden in the 1700s used a rectangular floor plan with six rooms, which developed from a French baroque plan. During the 1800s this plan also became more widespread among large farms. Some of the houses built at the religious colony of Bishop Hill, Ill., in the late 1840s have this floor plan, as well as a symmetrical facade.

Gradual changes in Swedish-American building traditions are illustrated in their evolution from small temporary early log buildings with almost symmetrical floor plans to later T- and L-shaped additions to stick and shingled designs with irregular floor plans, bay windows and porches. The development mirrored the change from temporary to permanent buildings as soon as a family could afford it. "Typical" Swedish houses are difficult to discern among old midwestern houses. The traditional floor plan often was still used, and wood was still the predominant building material, but the lumber was sawn

Sod house in Nebraska, 1886, a common housing solution on the prairie where trees for log houses were lacking. (Nordiska Museet)

into boards, often precut. The floor plan, the location of the
door and symmetrical placement of windows on the facade
have direct parallels in Swedish vernacular architecture.

Building the first barn in the new country required even
more teamwork than building the first house. Only a few
original log barns remain. Many Swedish barns seen today
in Minnesota were built in frame during the first decade of
this century. With the development of dairy herds, the need
for hay storage increased. The barn height was raised to
allow greater space, with the hayloft on top or beside the
cow barn. At the same time, larger barns with gambrel
roofs and later types with arched roofs became common;
both have the cow barn on the lower level and the hay mow
on top. Early gambrel-roof barns were sometimes built of
lumber from the farmer's property and with the help of
skilled carpenters who supervised the barn raising. Later
contractors and construction crews built both types of
barns with beams available in standard sizes from lumber
yards. While houses generally had horizontal siding painted
white, barns had vertical siding painted red.

Early Swedish-American farms in Minnesota, unlike

Small log cabin of the *enkelstuga*
type built by early Swedish
immigrants based on rural
Swedish traditions.

Lars Johannes Petterson family
outside their South Dakota home,
built in 1873 with a floor plan
similar to a *parstuga*. (Nordiska
Museet)

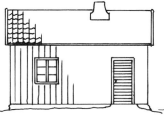

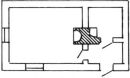

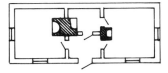

Traditional Swedish *enkelstuga*
with a side entrance, entry hall,
small storeroom or kitchen and
the *stuga* (all-purpose room).

Parstuga plan, a symmetrical two-
room cottage often created by
adding a room and an entrance
hall to a one-room cottage.

contemporary Swedish farms, did not have distinct plans. Swedish farms were organized in regional patterns closely related to the structure of the village. The long, rectangular-shaped farms in southeastern Sweden, for example, were well adapted to the one-street villages of this region. One reason these patterns were not repeated in Minnesota was that the early settlers did not have to adapt their farm buildings to an existing village.

Gothic-style wood churches can be found in parts of Minnesota settled by Swedes. These bear similarities with some white-painted frame churches in Sweden, although these are smaller and less common than the more typical neo-Gothic brick Swedish churches.

While the Swedes helped make the log cabin a potent image of frontier America, like other immigrants they adapted their traditions to the new environment and styles, generally building Scandinavian forms in American materials. ▨

Chisago County, Minn., house about 1890. The *parstuga* plan, open porch, windows and other details had parallels in Swedish vernacular architecture of the period. (Minnesota Historical Society)

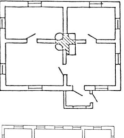

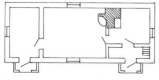
Framkammarstuga plan, another single-room house also known as a side-room cottage because of its room added to the *stuga*.

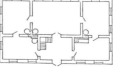
Four- and six-room plans, used in Sweden in the 1800s for larger houses that often had double rows of rooms.

Andersson House (c. 1870s),
Chisago County, Minn., recalling
southern Swedish buildings in its
long, narrow lines and steep roof
with a narrow projection. Its half-
timbering was filled with cement.
(Nordiska Museet)

Evolutionary type of Swedish-
American house, symmetrical
with a T- or L-shaped addition.

Barn in Chisago County, Minn.,
combining vertical and horizontal
siding. As in Sweden, vertical
siding, made of thicker and wider
boards sawn by hand, was most
common until about 1900.
Horizontal siding became more
popular when boards could be
purchased from local sawmills.
(Nordiska Museet)

Opposite: Mamrelund Lutheran
Church (1883), Kandiyohi County,
Minn., a Gothic Revival style
favored by Swedish-Americans.
(Nordiska Museet)

Assymmetrical house form adopted by Swedish immigrants during the Victorian era.

Carlson family at their South Dakota house about 1880. The house is a *parstuga* with additions forming a T-shaped plan. (Nordiska Museet)

UKRAINIANS
John C. Lehr

From the 1880s on, Ukrainian peasants from the Austrian-administered western Ukraine came to North America in search of land and opportunity. Before 1892 their destinations were the industrial regions of the U.S. eastern seaboard, where they were attracted by the opportunity for work in the factories and mines. Virtually all settled among other Slavic immigrants in urban centers, where they occupied existing housing; they thus had no opportunity to transfer their domestic architecture to North America. Only after 1892, when they began to seek homesteads on the agricultural frontier of the Canadian prairie provinces — Manitoba, Saskatchewan and Alberta — were they in a position to do so. Here, as pioneers, they created a new landscape, transplanting the domestic and religious architecture of their home provinces of Halychyna and Bukovyna to the North American West. Although a few small groups moved into North Dakota, settling in the Gorham, Ukraina and Wilton areas, their comparatively small numbers, as well as environmental and social factors, militated against the same degree of material culture transfer as took place in Canada.

St. Josaphat Ukrainian Catholic Church, Gorham, N.D., with parishioners gathered in front after the Sunday service in the late 1890s. (Ukrainian Museum, New York)

Before the outbreak of World War I in 1914 terminated emigration from central Europe, Canada received more than 170,000 Ukrainian immigrants. Most sought free homestead lands in the aspen parkland north of the open prairie, where they found the wood and water required to pursue subsistence agriculture and a physical environment similar to that of their homeland provinces in the Carpathian foothills. Their settlement has a distinctive geographical pattern — a series of massive blocks running in an arc from east-central Alberta into southeastern Manitoba with a few small scattered areas in North Dakota.

On the open prairie of North Dakota sod houses were used as temporary dwellings until replaced by conventional frame buildings. In Canada the first temporary shelters were dugouts roofed over with poplar logs and sod. These crude but effective structures housed family and stock until permanent dwellings were built. As a general rule in Canada, and occasionally in North Dakota, their houses were replicas of the dwellings left behind in the Ukraine, where building in wood had achieved a high level of competency and produced pleasing and practical dwellings.

Pièce sur pièce house, near Vita, Manitoba, being plastered with mud by Ukrainian immigrants in 1916. (Manitoba Archives)

Right: Abandoned house, near Caliento, Manitoba, revealing details of Ukrainian roof construction and thatching techniques. (John C. Lehr)

Petro Demianiw House, near Gorham, N.D., a Galician-style house constructed of wattle and daub. (William C. Sherman)

Opposite: Galician-style house (c. 1919), near Sheho, Saskatchewan, with the traditional hipped-gable thatched roof. (Saskatchewan Archives)

Below: Two common floor plans of Ukrainian houses — the two-room house with and without a central hall. (John C. Lehr)

Bukovynian-style house (c. 1911), near Gardenton, Manitoba, with flared log eaves brackets and heavy roof overhang. (John C. Lehr)

In the wooded environment of the western Ukraine, the folk tradition embraced three styles of log construction. The techniques reflected local timber prices and availability: horizontal log, if good logs were available; post and fill (or *pièce sur pièce*), if timber prices were high; and vertical logs of smaller diameter, if prices were prohibitive. All three methods were used in North America although the controlling factor was not price but the quality of timber present in each locality.

Ukrainian pioneer houses had distinct characteristics yet displayed a wide variation in their outward appearance. Virtually all were one-story log buildings with gabled, hipped-gable or hipped roofs. All faced south; the vast majority were plastered on the interior with mud and straw and had a white limewashed exterior. The arrangement of interior social space, including doors, windows, stove and chimney, varied little, revolving around a basic two-room format. The westernmost room, *mala khata* (little house), housed a large clay stove and was the center of household activity. The *velyka khata* (big house) was reserved for formal functions or used as the bedroom of the parents in a large family. On its eastern wall, the "holy" wall, were placed icons and religious calendars. Many Ukrainian houses initially had steeply pitched hipped or hipped-gable roofs. Later replacement of thatch by wood shingles was accompanied by a lowering of the pitch and the wide adoption of the simple gabled roof, with a pent extension placed on the gable end at the eaves level to deflect rainwater away from the plastered wall.

The buildings of immigrants from Bukovyna can be distinguished by their larger size, the frequent inclusion of a central hallway between the *mala khata* and *velyka khata* and a heavy roof with projecting eaves of up to four feet. On buildings of horizontal logs, the topmost logs were

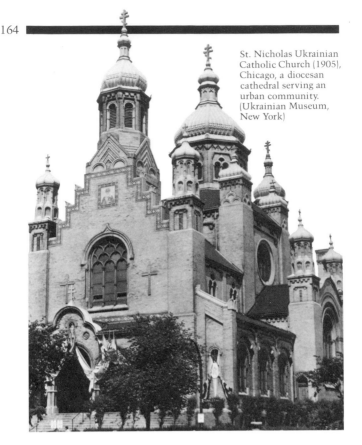

St. Nicholas Ukrainian Catholic Church (1905), Chicago, a diocesan cathedral serving an urban community. (Ukrainian Museum, New York)

flared out to form graceful eaves brackets, whose function was as much aesthetic as practical. Eyebrow vents, relics of the prechimney method of smoke dispersal, were another feature found exclusively on Bukovynian houses.

The Ukrainian folk house always remained a rural dwelling. Immigrants in the cities of western Canada and the eastern United States simply occupied existing housing and had little impact on the cultural landscape apart from introducing their distinctive Greek Orthodox and Greek Catholic churches.

Early Ukrainian churches in rural areas were of logs and, in the 1930s, of frame construction. They were distinguished by an eastward orientation, a blend of high style and folk elements, a Byzantine dome and cupolas, a separate bell tower and a tripartite division of interior space into porch, nave and sanctuary. Until recently the nave was open; pews and chairs are a post-1945 addition. Services were sung *a capella*; a raised balcony by the porch accommodated the choir. The *iconostas* (decorated screen) separated the sanctuary from the nave and, like the rest of the church decor, was rich in liturgical and spiritual symbolism.

Notable in church design was Father Philip Ruh (1883-1962), who built many churches across western Canada, interpreting Ukrainian church architecture in a distinctive fashion. Recently, Radoslav Zuk has conceptually embodied the traditional spirit of Ukrainian Catholic church architecture in his Holy Family Church (1962) in Winnipeg and Holy Trinity Ukrainian Catholic Church (1976) in Kerhonkson, N.Y. In his designs he has moved beyond simple replication of traditional forms to create a new religious architecture founded on the assumptions, traditions and aesthetics of the old. ▣

St. Michael's Church (1884), Shenandoah, Pa., the first Ukrainian Catholic church in America. (Ukrainian Museum, New York)

Ukrainian Pavilion (1933), Century of Progress World's Fair, Chicago, using traditional logs and massing. (Ukrainian Museum, New York)

Holy Trinity Church (1976, Radoslav Zuk; Gorman, Mixon and Blood), Kerhonkson, N.Y., combining traditional and contemporary Ukrainian architectural forms. (Radoslav Zuk)

Contributors

Charles F. Calkins is professor of geography and dean of the faculty at Carroll College, Waukesha, Wis. His research and publications on ethnic folk architecture range widely from the beehives of Costa Rica to the Pomeranian barns of Wisconsin.

Cary Carson is director of research at the Colonial Williamsburg Foundation, Williamsburg, Va. He writes social history using information from architectural field surveys and archeological excavations. He is currently working on a history of early American material life.

Thomas Carter is an architectural historian with the Utah Division of State History, Salt Lake City, and adjunct assistant professor in the Graduate School of Architecture at the University of Utah. His Danish research has been supported by the American-Scandinavian Foundation.

Edward A. Chappell is director of the Architectural Research Department at the Colonial Williamsburg Foundation, Williamsburg, Va. He began fieldwork on German buildings while a graduate student at the University of Virginia and has written several articles on Rhenish-American culture.

Kathleen Deagan is curator of historical archeology and chairperson of the Florida State Museum Anthropology Department, Gainesville. She has directed archeological research on Spanish sites in St. Augustine, Fla., and Haiti. Among her writings are *Spanish St. Augustine: The Archeology of a Colonial Cre-* *ole Community* and *Artifacts of the Spanish Colonies: Florida and the Caribbean.*

Bob Easton is an architect in Santa Barbara, Calif., and coauthor of the forthcoming *Native American Architecture.* He is also coauthor and designer of *Domebooks, Shelter* and *Santa Barbara Architecture.*

Jay D. Edwards is associate professor of anthropology at Louisiana State University, Baton Rouge. He is the author of several scholarly articles on West Indian and Louisiana architecture and of a forthcoming two-volume study of the vernacular architecture of French Louisiana. In the past 15 years he has conducted field studies in the West Indies, Louisiana, Missouri, Illinois, Quebec, England, Ireland and Normandy.

Henry Glassie is professor of folklore and American civilization at the University of Pennsylvania, Philadelphia. Among his major books are *Pattern in the Material Folk Culture of the Eastern United States, Folk Housing in Middle Virginia, Passing the Time in Ballymenone* and *Irish Folktales.*

Joe S. Graham is a member of the English Department at Texas A & M University, College Station. A specialist in Mexican-American folklore, he has done fieldwork and research in Texan-Mexican traditional and material cultures. He is now working on a book on Hispanic-American material culture in the United States.

Darrell D. Henning is a curator of the Norwegian-American Museum, Decorah, Iowa. He has studied traditional rural architecture in upstate New York and Long Island in connection with his work at Old Bethpage Village Restoration and has traveled throughout Norway and the Midwest studying Norwegian culture.

Matti Kaups is professor of geography and ethnohistory at the University of Minnesota, Duluth. A Fulbright scholar in Finland during 1986, he has written several articles on folk architecture of Finnish immigrants in the United States.

Michael Koop is survey coordinator for the Montana Historic Preservation Office, Helena. He is coauthor of *German-Russian Architecture in Southeastern South Dakota* and coproducer of the film *Folk Building of the South Dakota German-Russians.*

William G. Laatsch is professor of regional analysis and geography at the University of Wisconsin, Green Bay. He lives on the Door Peninsula, where he pursues his interest in rural settlement forms and patterns. He has contributed papers and articles to a variety of forums and currently serves on Wisconsin's Historic Preservation Review Board.

Ronald K. K. Lee, AIA, is a practicing architect in Honolulu, Hawaii. For 10 years he lectured in the Department of Architecture at the University of Hawaii, Manoa, on the history and theory of architecture.

John C. Lehr is associate professor in the Department of Geography at the University of Winnipeg, Manitoba. He is past president of the Society for the Study of Architecture in Canada and is vice chairman of the Historic Sites Advisory Board of the Province of Manitoba. His research interests focus on pioneer settlement of ethnic groups in western Canada, folk architecture and the evolution of cultural landscapes.

Ray Morris is an architect in Honolulu who has lived in Hawaii since 1926. His interest in native Hawaiian architecture led him to plan and build the Hawaiian Village in Hilo and to design reproduction Hawaiian houses for the Ulu Mau Village, built by the Honolulu Junior Chamber of Commerce.

David Murphy is Nebraska Historic Buildings Survey architect and acting deputy state historic preservation officer for the Nebraska State Historical Society, Lincoln. Active in recording vernacular buildings in the region for the past 12 years, his current focus is on Bohemian- and Moravian-American buildings.

Peter Nabokov is a predoctoral fellow at the Newberry Library, Chicago. He is the author of *Architecture of Acoma Pueblo: The 1934 Historic American Buildings Survey Project* and coauthor of the forthcoming *Native American Architecture.*

Lena A:son Palmqvist is curator at the Department of Field Research and Archives at Nordiska Museet, Stockholm, Sweden. She is responsible for projects on building history and preservation and has conducted fieldwork in Chisago and Kandiyohi counties, Minn., in 1981 and 1985.

Anatole Senkevitch, Jr., is associate professor in the College of Architecture at the University of Michigan, Ann Arbor, where he heads the graduate concentration in historic preservation. In addition to doing research in the Soviet Union as a member of the U.S. Historic Preservation Team and a senior Fulbright and IREX fellow, he has written and spoken on the early architecture of Russian America.

William H. Tishler is professor of landscape architecture at the University of Wisconsin, Madison, where he teaches courses in historic preservation. The designer of the master plan for Old World Wisconsin, the outdoor museum of ethnic culture, he has done extensive research on vernacular buildings in the upper Midwest. He is writing a book on the rural architecture of Wisconsin's many immigrant groups.

Dell Upton teaches architectural history at the University of California, Berkeley. He is the author of *Holy Things and Profane: Anglican Parish Churches in Colonial Virginia* and editor of *Common Places: Readings in American Vernacular Architecture* (with John Michael Vlach). He also serves as editor of the *Vernacular Architecture Newsletter.*

John Michael Vlach is associate professor of American studies and anthropology at the George Washington University, Washington, D.C., where he is director of the folklife program.

He is the author of *The Afro-American Tradition in Decorative Arts,* editor of *Common Places* with Dell Upton and *Folk Art and Art Worlds* with Simon Bronner and has researched African and Afro-American material culture in Nigeria, Ghana, Jamaica, Haiti and the southern United States, particularly South Carolina and Louisiana. Recently he was an NEH fellow at the Winterthur Museum.

Christopher Lee Yip is assistant professor of environmental design at the University of Colorado, Boulder, where he teaches design and architectural history. He has done research, lectured and published articles on San Francisco's Chinatown, rural Chinatowns in California and colonial settlement on the China coast.

Further Reading

This reading list concentrates on ethnic architecture and landscapes, and is arranged alphabetically by ethnic group. The first section lists works mentioned in the introduction, architectural works relevant to more than one ethnic group and nonarchitectural discussions of the theory of ethnicity, the history of immigration and ethnic relations, and the history and sociology of individual ethnic groups.

Introduction and General Sources

Byington, Margaret. *Homestead: The Households of a Mill Town.* 1910. Reprint. Pittsburgh: University Center for International Studies, University of Pittsburgh, 1974.

Cohen, Lizabeth A. "Embellishing a Life of Labor: An Interpretation of the Material Culture of American Working-Class Homes, 1885 – 1915." In *Common Places: Readings in American Vernacular Architecture,* edited by Dell Upton and John Michael Vlach. Athens: University of Georgia Press, 1986.

Erixon, Sigurd. "The North-European Technique of Corner Timbering," *Folk-Liv* 1(1937): 13 – 60.

"Ethnic Studies in America." Special issue of *American Quarterly* 33, no. 3(Bibliography 1981): 257 – 354.

Glassie, Henry. *Pattern in the Material Folk Culture of the Eastern United States.* Philadelphia: University of Pennsylvania Press, 1969.

———. "The Types of the Southern Mountain Cabin." In *The Study of American Folklore,* by Jan H. Brunvand. New York: W. W. Norton, 1968.

Hansen, Marcus Lee. *The Atlantic Migration, 1607 – 1860,* edited by Arthur M. Schlesinger. Cambridge: Harvard University Press, 1940.

Higham, John. *Strangers in the Land: Patterns of American Nativism, 1860 – 1925.* New Brunswick, N.J.: Rutgers University Press, 1963.

Hobsbawm, Eric, ed. *The Invention of Tradition.* Cambridge, England: Cambridge University Press, 1983.

Jordan, Terry G. *American Log Building: An Old World Heritage.* Chapel Hill: University of North Carolina Press, 1985.

Kniffen, Fred B., and Henry Glassie. "Building in Wood in the Eastern United States: A Time-Place Perspective." In *Common Places: Readings in American Vernacular Architecture,* edited by Dell Upton and John Michael Vlach. Athens: University of Georgia Press, 1986.

Luebke, Frederick C. "Ethnic Group Settlement on the Great Plains," *Western Historical Quarterly* 8, no. 4(1977): 405 – 30.

Noble, Allen G. "Rural Ethnic Islands." In *Ethnicity in Contemporary America: A Geographical Appraisal,* edited by Jesse O. McKee. Dubuque, Iowa: Kendall-Hunt Publishing Company, 1985.

Raitz, Karl B. "Themes in the Cultural Geography of European Ethnic Groups in the United States," *Geographical Review* 69, no. 1(January 1979): 79 – 94.

Staub, Shalom. "The Near East Restaurant: A Study of the Spatial Manifestation of the Folklore of Ethnicity," *New York Folklore* 7, nos. 1 – 2(Summer 1981): 113 – 27.

Teske, Robert Thomas. "Living Room Furnishings, Ethnic Identity, and Acculturation Among Greek-Philadelphians," *New York Folklore* 5, nos. 1 – 2 (Summer 1979): 21 – 31.

Thernstrom, Stephan, Ann Orlov and Oscar Handlin, eds. *Harvard Encyclopedia of American Ethnic Groups.* Cambridge: Harvard University Press, 1980. [The essential starting point for the study of ethnicity. Includes excellent short bibliographies on individual groups.]

Afro-Americans

Anthony, Carl. "The Big House and the Slave Quarters," Part I, *Landscape* 20, no. 3(1975), 8 – 19; Part II, *Landscape* 21, no. 1(1976), 9 – 15.

Denyer, Susan. *African Traditional Architecture: An Historical and Geographical Perspective.* New York: Holmes and Meier, 1978.

Georgia Writers Project. *Drums and Shadows: Survival Studies Among Georgia Coastal Negroes.* Athens: University of Georgia Press, 1940.

McDaniel, George W. *Hearth and Home: Preserving a People's Culture.* Philadelphia: Temple University Press, 1982.

Vlach, John Michael. "Affecting Architecture of the Yoruba," *African Arts* 10, no. 1(October 1976): 48 – 53.

_____. *The Afro-American Tradition in Decorative Arts.* Cleveland: Cleveland Museum of Art, 1978.

_____. "The Shotgun House: An African Architectural Legacy." In *Common Places: Readings in American Vernacular Architecture,* edited by Dell Upton and John Michael Vlach. Athens: University of Georgia Press, 1986.

Belgians

Calkins, Charles F., and William G. Laatsch. "The Belgian Outdoor Ovens of Northeastern Wisconsin," *Pioneer America Society Transactions* 2(1979): 1 – 12.

Kahlert, John, and Albert Quinlan. *Early Door County Buildings and the People Who Built Them, 1849 – 1910.* Baileys Harbor, Wis.: Meadow Lane Publishers, 1976.

Merenne, Emile, and Louis Thiernesse. *Maisons et villages de Wallonie.* Gembloux, Belgium: Editions J. Duculot, 1979.

Metzler, Lee W. "The Belgians in the North Country," *Wisconsin Magazine of History* 26(March 1943): 280 – 88.

Weyns, Jozef. *Bakhuis en broodbakken in Vlaanderen.* Sint Martens-Latem: Verbond Voor Heemkunde, 1963.

Chinese

Allen-Wheeler, Jane. "A Herbalist's Shop in Honolulu: Traditional Merchandising in a Modern Setting." In *Modern Material Culture: The Archaeology of Us,* edited by Richard A. Gould and Michael B. Schiffer. New York: Academic Press, 1981.

Arreola, Daniel D. "The Chinese Role in Creating the Early Cultural Landscape of the Sacramento-San Joaquin Delta," *California Geographer* 15(1975): 1 – 15.

Salter, Christopher L. *San Francisco's Chinatown: How Chinese a Town?* San Francisco: R and E Research Associates, 1978.

Yip, Christopher. "A Time for Bitter Strength: The Chinese in Locke, California," *Landscape* 22, no. 2(Spring 1978): 3 – 13.

Czechs

Jirasek, Alois. *Some Aspects of Czech Culture.* 1894. Translated by Richard Neuse. New Haven: Human Relations Area Files, 1953.

Kovářů, Věra. *Lidový Dům v Jihomoravskem Kraji.* Brno: Krajske Stredksko Statni Pamatkova Pece a Ochrany Prirody, 1976.

Salzmann, Zdenek, and Vladimir Scheufler. *Komarov: A Czech Farming Village.* New York: Holt, Rinehart and Winston, 1974.

Sanda, J., and M. Weatherall. "Czech Village Architecture," *Architectural Review* 109, no. 652(April 1951): 255 – 61.

Vavroušek, Boh., and Dra. Zdeňka Wirtha. *Dědina: 516 Fotgografií Lidovych Staveb v Republice Československe.* Prague: Vytiskla Průmyslová Tiskárna v Praze, 1925.

Danes

Betsinger, Signe Tronborg. *Danish Immigrant Homes: Glimpses from Southwestern Minnesota.* Miscellaneous Publication 38, Agricultural Experiment Station, University of Minnesota, 1986.

Christiansen, Palle Ove. "Peasant Adaptation to Bourgeois Culture? Class Formation and Cultural Revolution in the Danish Countryside," *Ethnologia Scandinavica 1978:* 98 – 152.

Jørgensen, Lisbet Balslev. *Danmarks Arkitektur: Enfamiliehuset.* Copenhagen: Gyldenhal, 1979.

Stoklund, Bjarne. *Bondegård og Byggeskik før 1850.* Copenhagen: Danks Historisk Faellestorenings Handboger, 1972.

———. "Landbygninger Til 1870." In *Danmarks Bygningskunst,* edited by Hakon Lund and Knud Millech. Copenhagen: H. Hirschsprings, 1963.

Dutch

Bailey, Rosalie Fellows. *Pre-Revolutionary Dutch Houses and Families in Northern New Jersey and Southern New York.* New York: Holland Society, 1936.

Fitchen, John F. *The New World Dutch Barn: A Study of Its Characteristics, Its Structural System, and Its Probable Erectional Procedures.* Syracuse: Syracuse University Press, 1968.

Fockema Andreae, S. J., E. H. ter Kuile and R. C. Hekker. *Duizen Jaar Bouwen in Nederland.* Amsterdam: Allert de Lange, 1957.

Jakle, John A., and James O. Wheeler. "The Changing Residential Structure of the Dutch Population in Kalamazoo, Michigan," *Annals of the Association of American Geographers* 59, no. 3(September 1969): 441 – 60.

Merwick, Donna. "Dutch Townsmen and Land Use: A Spatial Perspective on Seventeenth-Century Albany, New York," *William and Mary Quarterly* 37, no. 1 (January 1980): 53 – 78.

"New Netherland Studies: An Inventory of Current Research and Approaches." Special issue of *Bulletin KNOB* 84, nos. 2 – 3(June 1985): 46 – 180.

Prudon, Theodore H. M. "The New World Dutch Barn: Survival of a Medieval Structural Frame." In *Common Places: Readings in American Vernacular Architecture,* edited by Dell Upton and John Michael Vlach. Athens: University of Georgia Press, 1986.

Reynolds, Helen W. *Dutch Houses in the Hudson Valley Before 1776.* New York: Holland Society, 1929.

English

Carson, Cary, Norman F. Barka, William M. Kelso, Garry Wheeler Stone and Dell Upton. "Impermanent Architecture in the Southern American Colonies," *Winterthur Portfolio* 16, nos. 2 – 3 (Summer-Autumn 1981): 135 – 96.

Clark, Clifford Edward, Jr. *The American Family Home, 1800 – 1960.* Chapel Hill: University of North Carolina Press, 1986.

Cummings, Abbott Lowell. *The Framed Houses of Massachusetts Bay, 1625 – 1725.* Cambridge: Harvard University Press, 1979.

Hitchcock, Henry-Russell. *Architecture: Nineteenth and Twentieth Centuries.* Baltimore: Penguin Books, 1958. [See especially Chapter 15, "The Development of the Detached House in England and America from 1800 to 1900."]

Marshall, Howard Wight. *Folk Architecture in Little Dixie: A Regional Culture in Missouri.* Columbia: University of Missouri Press, 1981.

Mercer, Eric. *English Vernacular Houses: A Study of Traditional Farmhouses and Cottages.* London: Her Majesty's Stationery Office, 1975.

St. George, Robert Blair. "'Set Thine House in Order': The Domestication of the Yeomanry in Seventeenth-Century New England." In *Common Places: Readings in American Vernacular Architecture,* edited by Dell Upton and John Michael Vlach. Athens: University of Georgia Press, 1986.

Finns

Alanen, Arnold R., and William H. Tishler. "Finnish Farmstead Organization in Old and New World Settings," *Journal of Cultural Geography* 1, no. 1(Fall-Winter 1980): 66 – 81.

Glanville, Ranulph. "Finnish Vernacular Farmhouses," *Architectural Association Quarterly* 9, no. 1(1977): 36 – 52.

Kaups, Matti. "A Finnish Savusauna in Minnesota," *Minnesota History* 45(Spring 1976): 11 – 20.

_____. "Log Architecture in America: European Antecedents in a Finnish Context," *Journal of Cultural Geography* 2, no. 1(Fall-Winter 1981): 131 – 53.

_____. "Finnish Log Houses in the Upper Middle West: 1890 – 1920," *Journal of Cultural Geography* 3, no. 2(Spring-Summer 1983): 2 – 26.

Mather, Cotton, and Matti Kaups. "The Finnish Sauna: A Cultural Index to Settlement," *Annals of the Association of American Geographers* 53, no. 4(December 1963): 494 – 504.

French

Edwards, Jay D. "Cultural Syncretism in the Louisiana Creole Cottage," *Louisiana Folklore Miscellany* 4, no. 1(1980): 9 – 40.

_____. *Louisiana's French Vernacular Architecture: An Historical and Social Bibliography.* Architecture Series, A-1603. Monticello, Ill.: Vance Bibliographies, 1986.

Fitch, James Marston. "Creole Architecture, 1718 – 1860: The Rise and Fall of a Great Tradition." In *The Past as Prelude: New Orleans, 1718 – 1968,* edited by Hodding Carter. New Orleans: Pelican Publishing, 1968.

Gowans, Alan. *Church Architecture in New France.* Toronto: University of Toronto Press, 1955.

Kniffen, Fred B. "Louisiana House Types," *Annals of the Association of American Geographers* 26, no. 4(December 1936): 179 – 93.

Lessard, Michel, and Huguette Marquis. *Encyclopedie de la maison quebecoise: 3 siecles d'habitations.* Montreal: Les Editions de l'Homme, 1972.

Millar, Donald. "A Quaint Dutch Survival: The Jean Hasbrouck House, New Paltz, N.Y.," *Architectural Record* 59, no. 3(March 1926): 228 – 32. [Built by a French family.]

Moogk, Peter. *Building a House in New France: An Account of the Perplexities of Client and Craftsman in Early Canada.* Toronto: McClelland and Stewart, 1977.

Peterson, Charles E. *Colonial St. Louis: Building a Creole Capital.* St. Louis: Missouri Historical Society, 1949.

Post, Lauren C. *Cajun Sketches from the Prairies of Southwest Louisiana.* Baton

Rouge: Louisiana State University Press, 1962.

Séguin, Robert-Lionel. *Les granges du Québec du XVIIe au XIXe siècle.* Montreal: Les Editions Quinze, 1976.

Thurman, Melburn M. *Building a House in 18th Century Ste. Genevieve.* Ste. Genevieve, Mo.: Pendragon's Press, 1984.

Traquair, Ramsay. *The Old Architecture of Quebec.* Toronto: Macmillan, 1947.

Wilson, Samuel, Jr. "Architecture in Eighteenth Century West Florida." In *Eighteenth Century Florida and Its Borderlands,* edited by Samuel Proctor. Gainesville: University of Florida Press, 1975.

————. "Gulf Coast Architecture." In *Spain and Her Rivals on the Gulf Coast,* edited by Ernest F. Dibble and Earle W. Newton. Pensacola: Historic Pensacola Preservation Board, 1971.

German-Russians

Koop, Michael, and Stephen Ludwig. *German-Russian Folk Architecture in Southeastern South Dakota.* Vermillion, S.D.: State Historical Preservation Center, 1984.

Low, Robert. *Deutsche Bauernstuben auf russicher Steppe.* Berlin-Charlottenburg: Ostlandverlag, 1916.

Petersen, Albert J. "The German-Russian House in Kansas: A Study in Persistence of Form," *Pioneer America* 8, no. 1(January 1976): 19 – 27.

Sallet, Richard. *Russian-German Settlements in the United States.* Translated by Lavern J. Rippley and Armand Bauer. Fargo: North Dakota Institute for Regional Studies, 1974.

Germans

Baumgarten, Karl. *Das deutsche Bauernhaus.* Rev. ed. Berlin: Akademie-Verlag, 1985.

Bucher, Robert C. "The Swiss Bank House in Pennsylvania," *Pennsylvania Folklife* 18, no. 2(Winter 1968 – 69): 2 – 11.

Chappell, Edward. "Acculturation in the Shenandoah Valley: Rhenish Houses of the Massanutten Settlement," *Proceedings of the American Philosophical Society* 124, no. 1(February 1980): 55 – 89. Condensed in *Common Places: Readings in American Vernacular Architecture,* edited by Dell Upton and John Michael Vlach. Athens: University of Georgia Press, 1986.

Dornbusch, Charles H., and John K. Heyl. *Pennsylvania German Barns.* Published for the Pennsylvania German Society. Allentown, Pa.: Schlechter's, 1958.

Glassie, Henry. "Eighteenth-Century Cultural Process in Delaware Valley Folk Building." In *Common Places: Readings in American Vernacular Architecture,* edited by Dell Upton and John Michael Vlach. Athens: University of Georgia Press, 1986.

Jordan, Terry G. *German Seed in Texas Soil: Immigrant Farmers in Nineteenth-Century Texas.* Austin: University of Texas Press, 1966.

Marshall, Howard Wight. "'The Pelster House': Germanic Vernacular Building Traditions in Early Missouri." In *The German-American Experience in Missouri: Essays in Commemoration of the Tricentennial of German Immigration to America,* edited by Howard Wight Marshall and James W. Goodrich. Columbia: Missouri Cultural Heritage Center, University of Missouri, 1986.

————. "The Pelster Housebarn: Endurance of Germanic Architecture on the Midwestern Frontier," *Material Culture* 18, no. 2 (Summer 1986).

Murtagh, William. *Moravian Architecture and Town Planning: Bethlehem, Pennsylvania, and Other Eighteenth-Century American Settlements.* Chapel Hill: University of North Carolina Press, 1967.

Perrin, Richard W. E. *Historic Wisconsin Buildings: A Survey of Pioneer Architecture.* Milwaukee: Milwaukee Public Museum, 1981.

Swank, Scott T., with Benno M. Forman, Frank H. Sommer, Arlene Palmer Schwind, Frederick S. Weiser, Donald L. Fennimore and Susan Burrows Swan. *Arts of the Pennsylvania Germans.* Edited by Catherine E. Hutchins. New York: W. W. Norton, 1983.

Tishler, William H. "Fachwerk Construction in the German Settlements of Wisconsin," *Winterthur Portfolio* 21, no. 4 (Winter 1986).

Van Ravenswaay, Charles. *The Arts and Architecture of German Settlements in Missouri.* Columbia: University of Missouri Press, 1977.

Weiss, Richard. *Häuser und Landschaften der Schweiz.* 2d ed. Erlenbach-Zurich: Eugen Rentsch Verlag, 1973.

Wilhelm, Hubert G. H. "German Settlement and Folk Building Practices in the Hill Country of Texas," *Pioneer America* 3, no. 2 (July 1971): 15–24.

Hispanics: Spanish and Mexicans

Baer, Kurt, and Hugo Rudinger. *Architecture of the California Missions.* Berkeley: University of California Press, 1958.

Boyd, E. *Popular Arts of Spanish New Mexico.* Santa Fe: Museum of New Mexico Press, 1974.

Bunting, Bainbridge. *Early Architecture of New Mexico.* Albuquerque: University of New Mexico Press, 1976.

Feduchi, Luis. *Itinerarios de Arquitectura Popular Española.* 4 vols. Barcelona: Editorial Blume, 1974. [Volume one translated as *Spanish Folk Architecture.* New York: Editorial Blume, 1977.]

Flores, Carlos. *Arquitectura Popular Española.* 5 vols. Madrid: Editorial Aguilar, 1973–77.

Jackson, J. B. *Landscape Autoguide I: Santa Fe to Taos.* Santa Fe: *Landscape Magazine*, 1962.

_____. *Landscape Autoguide II: Santa Fe to the Upper Espanola Valley.* Santa Fe: *Landscape Magazine*, 1963.

_____. *Landscape Autoguide III: Santa Fe to Pecos and Villanueva.* Santa Fe: *Landscape Magazine*, 1963.

Kubler, George. *The Religious Architecture of New Mexico in the Colonial Period Since the American Occupation.* 1940. Reprint. Albuquerque: University of New Mexico Press, 1973.

Manucy, Albert. *The Houses of St. Augustine.* St. Augustine: St. Augustine Historical Society, 1962.

_____. "The Physical Setting of Sixteenth Century St. Augustine," *Florida Anthropologist* 35, nos. 1–2 (1958): 34–53.

Mendieta y Núñez, Lucio. *La habitacion indigena.* Mexico City: Imprenta Universitaria, 1939.

Newcomb, Rexford. *Spanish-Colonial Architecture in the United States.* New York: J. J. Augustin, 1937.

Sanford, Trent Elwood. *The Architecture of the Southwest.* 2d ed. New York: W. W. Norton, 1971.

Weitze, Karen J. *California's Mission Revival.* Los Angeles: Hennessey and Ingalls, 1984.

West, Robert C. "The Flat-Roofed Folk Dwelling in Rural Mexico." In *Man and Cultural Heritage: Essays in Honor of Fred B. Kniffen,* edited by H. J. Walker and W. G. Haag. Baton Rouge: Louisiana State University Press, 1974.

Irish

Danaher, Kevin. *Ireland's Vernacular Architecture.* Published for the Cultural Relations Committee of Ireland. Cork: Mercier Press, 1975.

Evans, E. Estyn. *Irish Folk Ways.* New York: Devin-Adair, 1957.

Gailey, Alan. *Rural Houses of the North of Ireland.* Edinburgh: John Donald, 1984.

Glassie, Henry. *Passing the Time in Ballymenone: Culture and History of an Ulster Community.* Philadelphia: University of Pennsylvania Press, 1982.

Mannion, John J. *Irish Settlements in Eastern Canada: A Study of Cultural Transfer and Adaptation.* Toronto: University of Toronto Press, 1974.

Welsch, Roger L. *Sod Walls: The Story of the Nebraska Sod House.* Broken Bow, Neb.: Purcells, 1968.

Japanese

DeFrancis, John. *Things Japanese in Hawaii.* Honolulu: University Press of Hawaii, 1973.

Fellows, Donald K. "Japanese Buddhism: Its Imprint on the California Landscape," *California Geographer* 13 (1972): 49–58.

Lancaster, Clay. *The Japanese Influence in America.* 1963. Reprint. New York: Abbeville Press, 1983.

Morse, Edward S. *Japanese Homes and Their Surroundings.* 1886. Reprint. Rutland, Vt.: Charles E. Tuttle, 1972.

Nishi, Kazuo, and Kazuo Hozumi. *What Is Japanese Architecture?* Translated by H. Mack Horton. Tokyo: Kodansha International, 1985.

Paine, Robert, and Alexander Soper. *The Art and Architecture of Japan.* London: Penguin Books, 1955.

Yoshida, Tetsuro. *The Japanese House and Garden.* New York: Praeger, 1969.

Native Americans

Jett, Stephen C., and Virginia Spencer. *Navajo Architecture: Forms, History, Distribution.* Tucson: University of Arizona Press, 1981.

Morgan, Lewis H. *Houses and House Life of the American Aborigines.* 1881. Reprint. Chicago: University of Chicago Press, 1965.

Morgan, William H. *Prehistoric Architecture of the Eastern United States.* Cambridge: MIT Press, 1980.

Nabokov, Peter. *Architecture of Acoma Pueblo: The 1934 Historic American Buildings Survey Project.* Santa Fe: Ancient City Press, 1986.

Native Hawaiians

Apple, Russell A. *City of Refuge National Historic Park: Hawaiian Thatched Houses. Use—Construction—Adaptation.* San Francisco: Office of History and Historic Architecture, National Park Service, 1971.

Hiroa, Te Rangi [Peter H. Buck]. *Arts and Crafts in Hawaii.* Honolulu: Bernice P. Bishop Museum, 1957.

Hooili, J. "Construction of Houses in Hawaii Nei." In *Collection of Hawaiian Antiquities and Folk-lore,* compiled by Abraham Fornander. Honolulu: Bernice P. Bishop Museum, 1919.

Kirch, Patrick Vinton. *Feathered Gods and Fishhooks: An Introduction to Hawaiian Archaeology and Prehistory.* Honolulu: University of Hawaii Press, 1985.

Malo, David. *Hawaiian Antiquities.* 1898. Translated by Nathaniel B. Emerson. 2d ed. Honolulu: Bernice P. Bishop Museum, 1951.

Morris, Ray. "The Hawaiian House: Development of a Unique House Form," *Hawaii Architect* 8, no. 12 (December 1979): 3–33.

Norwegians

Henning, Darrell D. "Survival and Revival: Norwegian Material Culture." In *Passing Time and Traditions,* edited by Steve Ohrn. Published for the Iowa

Arts Council. Ames: Iowa State University Press, 1984.

Nelson, Marion J. "Material Culture and Folk Arts of the Norwegians in America." In *Perspectives in American Folk Art*, edited by Ian M. G. Quimby and Scott T. Swank. Published for the Henry Francis du Pont Winterthur Museum. New York: W. W. Norton, 1980.

Peterson, Fred W. "Norwegian Farm Homes in Steele and Traill Counties, North Dakota: The American Dream and Retention of Roots, 1890 – 1914," *North Dakota History* 51, no. 1 (Winter 1984): 4 – 13.

Russians

Fedorova, Svetlana G. *The Russian Population in Alaska and California, Late 18th Century – 1867.* Translated by Richard A. Pierce and Alton S. Donnelly. Kingston, Ontario: Limestone Press, 1973.

Gibson, James R. *Imperial Russia in Frontier America: The Changing Geography of Supply of Russian America, 1784 – 1867.* New York: Oxford University Press, 1976.

Schwartz, Harvey. "Fort Ross, California: Imperial Russian Outpost on America's Western Frontier, 1812 – 1841," *Journal of the West* 18, no. 2 (1979): 35 – 48.

Senkevitch, Anatole, Jr. "The Early Architecture and Settlements of Russian America." In *Russia's American Colony*, edited by S. Frederick Starr. Durham: Duke University Press, 1986.

Spencer-Hancock, Diane, and William E. Pritchard. "The Chapel at Fort Ross: Its History and Reconstruction," *California History* 61, no. 1 (Spring 1982): 2 – 17.

Swedes

Erixon, Sigurd. *Svensk Byggnadskultur: Studier och skildringar belysande den svenska byggnaskulturens historia.* 1947. Reprint. Stockholm: Walter Ekstrand Bokfäg, 1982.

Palmqvist, Lena A:son. *Building Traditions Among Swedish Settlers in Rural Minnesota: Material Culture Relecting Persistence or Decline of Traditions.* Stockholm: Nordiska Museet, 1983.

Ukrainians

Hunter, Robert. "Ukrainian-Canadian Folk Architecture: The Churches of Father Philip Ruh." In *Selected Papers 5.* Ottawa: Society for the Study of Architecture in Canada, 1983.

Lehr, John C. *Ukrainian Vernacular Architecture in Alberta.* Edmonton: Alberta Culture, Historical Resources Division, 1976.

_____. "The Log Buildings of Ukrainian Settlers in Western Canada," *Prairie Forum* 5, no. 2 (1980): 183 – 96.

_____. "The Landscape of Ukrainian Settlement in the Canadian West," *Great Plains Quarterly* 2, no. 2 (Spring 1982): 94 – 105.

Wonders, William C. "Log Buildings of West Central Alberta," *Prairie Forum* 5, no. 2 (1980): 197 – 218.

Zuk, Radoslav. "Architectural Significance and Culture," *Canadian Ethnic Studies* 16, no. 3 (1984): 16 – 26.

Information Sources

Because ethnic architecture represents a relatively new and specialized area of study, organizations that are directly involved in this field and able to provide information to the public are few in number. One of the best sources of information on sites within a state is the state historic preservation office. Other organizations to contact for general information include state historical societies, state archives, state libraries and universities. The sources of assistance listed below should be able to provide background information on specific ethnic groups as well as on the general topic of vernacular architecture, immigration, historical settlement patterns and related issues.

General

Association of American Geographers
1710 16th Street N.W.
Washington, D.C. 20009

The Balch Institute
18 South Seventh Street
Philadelphia, Pa. 19106

Immigration History Research Center
University of Minnesota
826 Berry Street
St. Paul, Minn. 55114

National Museum of American History
Smithsonian Institution
Constitution Avenue Between 12th and 14th Streets, N.W.
Washington, D.C. 20560

Old World Wisconsin
Route 2, Box 18
Eagle, Wis. 53119

Pioneer America Society
Department of Geography
University of Akron
Akron, Ohio 44325

Vernacular Architecture Forum
c/o Maryland Historical Trust
21 State Circle
Annapolis, Md. 21401

Afro-Americans

Afro-American Heritage Association
P.O. Box 451
Rome, N.Y. 13440

Afro-American Historical and Cultural Museum
7th and Arch Streets
Philadelphia, Pa. 19106

Association for the Study of Afro-American Life and History
1409 14th Street, N.W.
Washington, D.C. 20005

Banneker-Douglas Museum of Afro-American Life and History
84 Franklin Street
Annapolis, Md. 21401

Black Archives Research Center and Museum
P.O. Box 809
Florida A & M University
Tallahassee, Fla. 32307

New York Public Library
Schomburg Center for Research in Black Culture
515 Lenox Avenue
New York, N.Y. 10037

Belgians

Belgian-American Ethnic Resource Collection
Special Collections Department
University of Wisconsin
Green Bay, Wis. 54301

Center for Belgian Culture of Western Illinois
712 18th Avenue
Moline, Ill. 61265

Chinese

China Institute in America
125 East 65th Street
New York, N.Y. 10021

Chinese American Cultural
Association
8122 Mayfield
Chesterland, Ohio 44026

Chinese Culture Foundation of
San Francisco
750 Kearny Street, 3rd Floor
San Francisco, Calif. 94108

Chinese Historical Society of
America
17 Adler Place
San Francisco, Calif. 14133

Chinese Historical Society
of Southern California
1648 Redcliff Street
Los Angeles, Calif. 90026

Hawaii Chinese History
Center
111 North King Street
Room 410
Honolulu, Hawaii 96817

Czechs

Archives of the Czechs and
Slovaks Abroad
University of Chicago Library
1100 East 57th Street
Chicago, Ill. 60637

Czech Heritage Foundation
P.O. Box 761
Cedar Rapids, Iowa 52406

Czechoslovak Heritage
Museum and Library
2701 South Harlem Avenue
Berwyn, Ill. 60402

Western Fraternal Life
Association
1900 First Avenue, N.E.
Cedar Rapids, Iowa 52402

Wilber Czech Museum
102 West 3rd Street
P.O. Box 253
Wilber, Nev. 68465

Danes

Danish-American Heritage
Society
29672 Dane Lane
Junction City, Ore. 97448

Danish Immigrant Museum
P.O. Box 178
Elk Horn, Iowa 51531

Grand View College Library
1200 Grandview Avenue
Des Moines, Iowa 50316

Dutch

Albany Institute of History
and Art
125 Washington Avenue
Albany, N.Y. 12210

Association for the
Advancement of Dutch-
American Studies
Calvin Library
3207 Burton, S.E.
Grand Rapids, Mich. 49506

Holland Society of New York
122 East 58th Street
New York, N.Y. 10022

Netherlands Museum
8 East 12th Street
Holland, Mich. 49423

New York Historical Society
170 Central Park West
New York, N.Y. 10024

English

Colonial Williamsburg
Foundation
P.O. Box C
Williamsburg, Va. 23185

Institute of Early American
History and Culture
Box 220
Williamsburg, Va. 23185

Old Sturbridge Village
Route 20
Sturbridge, Mass. 01566

Pennsbury Manor
400 Memorial Road
Morrisville, Pa. 19067

Plimoth Plantation
P.O. Box 1620
Plymouth, Mass. 02061

Society for the Preservation of
New England Antiquities
141 Cambridge Street
Boston, Mass. 02114

Strawbery Banke
P.O. Box 300
Portsmouth, N.H. 03801

Finns

Finnish-American Archives
Suomi College
Hancock, Mich. 49930

Finnish-American Historical
Society of Michigan
19885 Melrose
Southfield, Mich. 48075

Finnish-American Society
of the West
P.O. Box 3515
Portland, Ore. 97208

Suomi Conference of the
Lutheran Church in America
516 Villa Verde
Rio Rancho, N.M. 87124

French

C.E.L.A.T.
Université Laval
Quebec City, Quebec G1K 7P4,
Canada

Franco-American Heritage
Center
P.O. Box 1251
Lewiston, Maine 04240

French Library in Boston
53 Marlborough Street
Boston, Mass. 02116

Louisiana State Museum
Archives
400 Esplanade Avenue
New Orleans, La. 70116

National Federation of Franco-
American Genealogical and
Historical Societies
P.O. Box 3558
Manchester, N.H. 03105

Société Historique Franco-
Americaine
1 Social Street, Box F
Woonsocket, R.I. 02895

German-Russians

American Historical Society of
Germans from Russia
631 D Street
Lincoln, Neb. 68502

Germans from Russia Heritage
Society
1008 East Central Avenue
Bismarck, N.D. 58501

Germans from Russia in
Colorado Study Project
Colorado State University
History Department
Fort Collins, Colo. 80523

Institute for Regional Studies
North Dakota State
University
Fargo, N.D. 58102

Germans

Concordia Historical Institute
801 De Mun Avenue
St. Louis, Mo. 63105

Frankenmuth Historical
Museum
613 South Main
Frankenmuth, Mich. 48734

Goethe Institute German
Cultural Center
401 North Michigan Avenue
Chicago, Ill. 60611

Max Kade Institute for
German-American Studies
University of Wisconsin
Madison, Wis. 53706

Missouri Cultural Heritage
Center
University of Missouri
Columbia, Mo. 65211

Pennsylvania Folklore Society
P.O. Box 92
Collegeville, Pa. 19426

Pennsylvania-German Society
Box 397
Birdsboro, Pa. 19508

Old Salem
Drawer F, Salem Station
Winston-Salem, N.C. 27108

Winedale Historical Center
P.O. Box 11
FM Road 2714
Round Top, Tex. 78954

Hispanics: Spanish and Mexican

Biblioteca Latino Americana
Oakland Public Library
1900 Fruitvale Avenue, 1-A
Oakland, Calif. 94601

Hispanic Society of America
Broadway Between 155th and
156th Streets
New York, N.Y. 10032

Historic Pensacola
Preservation Board
205 East Zaragoza
Pensacola, Fla. 32501

Historic St. Augustine
Preservation Board
P.O. Box 1987
St. Augustine, Fla. 32085

Institute of Texan Cultures
Hemisfair Plaza
P.O. Box 1226
San Antonio, Tex. 78294

Latin American Library
Tulane University
Howard-Tilton Library
7001 Freret
New Orleans, La. 70118

Millicent Rogers Museum
P.O. Box A
Taos, N.M. 87571

National Hispanic Museum
421 North Avenue 19
P.O. Box 875377
Fourth Floor
Los Angeles, Calif. 90087

Old Cienega Village Museum
Route 2, Box 214
Santa Fe, N.M. 87501

Plaza de la Raza
3540 North Mission Road
Los Angeles, Calif. 90031

St. Augustine Historical
Society
271 Charlotte Street
St. Augustine, Fla. 32084

Shattuck Library
75A Newbury Street
Boston, Mass. 02116

Southwest Museum
P.O. Box 128
Highland Park Station
Los Angeles, Calif. 90042

Taylor Museum of the
Colorado Springs Fine Arts
Center
30 West Dale
Colorado Springs, Colo. 90903

Irish

American Committee for
Irish Studies
University of Wisconsin
Department of English
Milwaukee, Wis. 53201

American Irish Historical
Society
991 Fifth Avenue
New York, N.Y. 10028

Bapst Library
Special Irish Collection
Boston College
Chestnut Hill Branch
Boston, Mass. 02167

Irish American
Culture Institute
683 Osceola
St. Paul, Minn. 55105

Irish Cultural Society
106 Little Falls Street
Falls Church, Va. 22046

United Irish Cultural Center
2700 45th Avenue
San Francisco, Calif. 94116

Japanese

Asia Society
725 Park Avenue
New York, N.Y. 10021

Bernice P. Bishop Museum
Hawaii Immigrant Heritage
Preservation Center
1525 Bernice Street
P.O. Box 19000-A
Honolulu, Hawaii 96817

Historic Hawaii Foundation
119 Merchant Street, Suite 402
Honolulu, Hawaii 96813

Morikami Museum of
Japanese Culture
4000 Morikami Park Road
Delray Beach, Fla. 33446

Native Americans

Anchorage Historical and Fine
Arts Museum
121 West Seventh Avenue
Anchorage, Alaska 99502

California State Indian
Museum
2618 K Street
Sacramento, Calif. 95816

Indian and Colonial Research
Center
Main Street
Old Mystic, Conn. 06372

Museum of Indian Heritage
6040 DeLong Road
Eagle Creek Park
Indianapolis, Ind. 46254

Museum of Native American
Cultures
200 East Cataldo
P.O. Box 3044
Spokane, Wash. 99220

Museum of the American
Indian
Heye Foundation
Broadway at 155th Street
New York, N.Y. 10032

Native American Resource
Center
Pembroke State University
Pembroke, N.C. 28372

Native Hawaiians

Bernice P. Bishop Museum
1525 Bernice Street
P.O. Box 19000-A
Honolulu, Hawaii 96817

Hawaiian Historical Society
560 Kawaiahao Street
Honolulu, Hawaii 96813

Historic Hawaii Foundation
119 Merchant Street, Suite 402
Honolulu, Hawaii 96813

Kamehameha Schools
Hawaiian Studies Institute
Kapalama Heights
Honolulu, Hawaii 96817

Office of Hawaiian Affairs
Culture Office
567 South King Street
Suite 100
Honolulu, Hawaii 96813

University of Hawaii at Manoa
Hawaiian Studies Program
2424 Maile Way
Porteus 431
Honolulu, Hawaii 96816

Norwegians

Norskedalen
P.O. Box 225
Coon Valley, Wis. 54623

Norwegian-American
Historical Association
c/o St. Olaf College
Northfield, Minn. 55057

Sons of Norway
1455 West Lake Street
Minneapolis, Minn. 55408

Valdres Samband
Route No. 3, Box 86
Granite Falls, Minn. 56241

Vesterheim
Norwegian-American
Museum
502 West Water Street
Decorah, Iowa 52101

Russians

Alaska Department of Natural
Resources
Division of Parks
Office of History and
Archaeology

619 Warehouse Avenue
Suite 210
Anchorage, Alaska 99501

Fort Ross State Historical Park
19005 Coast Highway 1
Jenner, Calif. 95450

Kodiak Historical Society
Museum
Box 61
Kodiak, Alaska 99615

Sitka Historical Society
Museum
Centennial Building
P.O. Box 2414
Sitka, Alaska 99835

Sitka National Historical Park
Box 738
Sitka, Alaska 99835

Swedes

American Swedish Historical
Museum
1900 Pattison Avenue
Philadelphia, Pa. 19145

American Swedish Institute
2600 Park Avenue
Minneapolis, Minn. 55407

Emigrant Institute
Box 201
35104 Vaxjo, Sweden

Nordiska Museet
Djurgardsvagen 6-16
S-11521 Stockholm, Sweden

Swedish-American Historical
Society
5125 North Spaulding
Chicago, Ill. 60625

Swedish Historical Society
404 3rd Street
Rockford, Ill. 61108

Swiss

Swiss Community Historical
Society
Route 1
Pandora, Ohio 45877

Swiss Historical Village
Sixth and Seventh Streets
New Glarus, Wis. 53574

Tinker Swiss Cottage
411 Kent Street
Rockford, Ill. 11026

Ukrainians

Institute of Ukrainian Studies
University of Alberta
Edmonton, Alberta T6G 2J4,
Canada

Ukrainian Canadian Research
Foundation
4 Island View Boulevard
Toronto, Ontario M8V 2P4,
Canada

Ukrainian Cultural and
Educational Centre
184 Alexander Avenue East
Winnipeg, Manitoba R3B OL6,
Canada

Ukrainian Cultural Heritage
Village
c/o Alberta Culture
Historic Sites Service
8820 112th Street
Edmonton, Alberta T6G 2P8,
Canada

Ukrainian Heritage
Association and Museum of
Canada
1 Austin Terrace
Casa Loma
Toronto, Ontario M5R 1X8,
Canada

Ukrainian Museum
203 Second Avenue
New York, N.Y. 10021

Ukrainian Museum-Archives
1202 Kenilworth Avenue
Cleveland, Ohio 44113

Ukrainian Museum of Canada
910 Spadina Crescent, East
Saskatoon, Saskatchewan S7K
3H5, Canada

Ukrainian National Museum
2453 West Chicago Avenue
Chicago, Ill. 60622

Index

Other Books from The Preservation Press

GOODBYE HISTORY, HELLO HAMBURGER: AN ANTHOLOGY OF ARCHITECTURAL DELIGHTS AND DISASTERS. Ada Louise Huxtable. Foreword by John B. Oakes. These 68 pieces, most originally published in the *New York Times,* cover the classic urban confrontations of the 1960s and 1970s, analyzing the failures and successes and urging us to create more livable cities. 208 pp., illus., index. $14.95 pb.

HOUSES BY MAIL: A GUIDE TO HOUSES FROM SEARS, ROEBUCK AND COMPANY. Katherine Cole Stevenson and H. Ward Jandl. A unique history and guide to nearly 450 precut house models sold by Sears from 1908 to 1940, from bungalows to colonials, capturing the pride and memories of Sears house owners. 365 pp., illus., biblio., index. $24.95 pb.

INDUSTRIAL EYE. Photographs by Jet Lowe from the Historic American Engineering Record. Introduction by David Weitzman. More than 120 color and duotone photographs are featured in this album of an industrial America that few people have seen — famous landmarks such as the Statue of Liberty as well as less celebrated bridges, power plants, windmills and dams. 128 pp., illus., biblio. $34.95 hb.

RESPECTFUL REHABILITATION: ANSWERS TO YOUR QUESTIONS ABOUT OLD BUILDINGS. National Park Service. A "Dear Abby" for old buildings, this handy guide (now in an updated edition) answers 150 of the most-asked questions about rehabilitating old houses and other historic buildings. 200 pp., illus., biblio., index. $12.95 pb.

To order Preservation Press books, send the total of the book prices (less 10 percent discount for National Trust members), plus $3 postage and handling to: Preservation Shop, 1600 H Street, N.W., Washington, D.C. 20006. Residents of California, Colorado, Washington, D.C., Illinois, Iowa, Louisiana, Maryland, Massachusetts, New York, Pennsylvania, South Carolina, Texas and Virginia please add applicable sales tax. Make checks payable to the National Trust or provide your credit card number, expiration date, signature and telephone number.